HALLOWEEN

HALLOWEEN

An American Holiday, an American History

Lesley Pratt Bannatyne

Lesley Barfre

10/98

PELICAN PUBLISHING COMPANY

Gretna 1998

Published by Facts On File, Inc., 1990
Published by arrangement with the author by
Pelican Publishing Company, Inc., 1998

First Pelican edition, August 1998

Library of Congress Cataloging-in-Publication Data

Bannatyne, Lesley Pratt.
    Halloween : an American holiday, an American history / Lesley Pratt Bannatyne.—1st Pelican ed.
        p. cm.
    Originally published: New York : Facts on File, 1990.
    Includes bibliographical references and index.
    ISBN 1-56554-346-7 (pbk. : alk. paper)
    1. Halloween—United States.   2. United States—Social life and customs.   I. Title.
    GT4965.B28 1998
    394.2646—dc21   98-30160
                                                              CIP

Manufactured in the United States of America
Published by Pelican Publishing Company, Inc.
1000 Burmaster Street, Gretna, Louisiana 70053

For my family

Hallowe' en, Hallowe' en—
Strangest sights I' ve ever seen,
Witches hat, coal-black cats
Ghosts and gobblins,
Mice and rats.

—Author unknown

Contents

Introduction   ix

Chapter 1   A Blending of Traditions   1

Chapter 2   Forerunners to Halloween in the
American Colonies   19

Chapter 3   An Autumnal Feast in the New Nation   51

Chapter 4   The Immigration Years: Old World Customs in
Melting Pot America   65

Chapter 5   Halloween in Victorian America   99

Chapter 6   Halloween in the 20th Century   121

Chapter 7   Contemporary Halloween: Old Traditions
Made New   141

Bibliography   161

Index   175

Acknowledgments

I would like to thank the many people who helped during the research and writing of this book. I would especially like to express my gratitude to Meg Ruley, friend and agent, who initiated this project; to Neal Maillet and Kate Kelly, editors, for all their good work; to John Bay for his advice and r ding; to Liz Korabek for her library research; and to Doug Lipman, Cortlandt Hull, Diana Appelbaum, Jeanne Fleming and Margot Adler for their insight and assistance. I would also like to thank the staff of the Boston Public Library for their professionalism and patience during the course of my research there.

Introduction

It is Halloween. Grinning under a coal-black cat's head made of your mother's tights and pipe-cleaner whiskers, you ring your neighbor's doorbell. A porch light switches on and a shadowy figure opens the door. You stand your ground, heart pounding madly, and thrust out a brown paper bag. "Trick or treat!" The figure shies away in mock horror and returns to pop a chocolate in your bag. You fade back into the night, on to spook another house.

You might remember a similar encounter on Halloween as a child. Those born earlier in this century might remember a parade, or a barn dance with hot apple cider and fresh doughnuts. Our great-grandmothers would have conjured a different affair—a party, perhaps, with parlor games and roasted nuts and tubs filled with apples they'd fish for with a fork between their teeth. Earlier still, women might have gathered together in the farmhouse kitchen to ask if witches really do take the shape of bugs and pass through the keyholes of locked rooms…if bats really do eat the souls of the dead…or if you can really hear the devil read from the church steps the names of the ones who will die on Halloween. The history of Halloween in America is the history of American folk; it tells the story of the ethnic, religious and occult heritage of all the peoples who settled here.

You can trace the history of Halloween only if you define the celebration as a grouping of essential elements: communion with the ancestral dead, divination and fire. Witches, cats and bats. Pumpkins, pranks and masks. Costumes, tricks and treats. This is what Halloween is made of, a folk celebration that has endured and evolved from generation to generation.

Halloween begins well over 2,000 years ago in the British Isles. Here, we find the holiday stripped to its most essential element: a night when Celtic tribes communed with the spirits of the ancestral dead. These grand

and glorious pagan celebrations were assimilated by the Catholic church after the Romans conquered the lands of the Celts. Rather than extinguish old customs, the church leaders provided Christian versions of them: from the Middle Ages on, All Saints' Day and All Souls' Day replaced the ancient Celtic celebrations of the dead. These feast days, grouped with the eve of All Saints as Hallowmas, existed in Europe together with old pagan rituals for hundreds of years.

It was a tenuous connection at best that brought the seeds of Halloween to America. Whereas the holiday was once part of the seasonal folk culture of Europe, it was deemed political suicide for the 17th-century English Protestants—the Puritans—who immigrated to the northeastern part of America. The public celebration of Halloween disappeared in Puritan New England, but some of the holiday's folk elements traveled forward a few days in the calendar to a secular holiday, Guy Fawkes Day. Other American regions retained the celebration of All Saints' Day, and men and women in every colony acknowledged the occult elements associated with the holiday.

After the American Revolution, entertainments called play parties grew popular in the new, democratic nation. These were nondenominational public events that usually took place in local schoolhouses or town buildings rather than churches. People clapped and shouted, played games and told stories well into the night. The play party held in the late autumn was a precursor to American Halloween—there were apples and nuts aplenty, plus divination and dancing designed to encourage a little romance before the onslaught of a solitary rural winter.

But Halloween was still not a uniform, annual national celebration, like Thanksgiving or the Fourth of July, and its celebrations varied depending on the ethnic or regional heritage of its participants. Southern girls might look down a well to spy the face of their future husbands, while girls in Chicago wrapped eggs in string and watched them burn in the fire. Halloween in the Northeast might have been a toasty gathering around a fire with celebrants eating nuts and telling stories; in the Ozarks, Halloween might have been a barn dance and a grinning contest.

A real synthesis of Halloween customs did not take place until the mid-19th century, when famine in Ireland drove many thousands to America to find new homes. The Irish had precious little to pack with them in the way of wealth or belongings, but they did manage to bring along their old-world October 31st celebration. Wherever the Irish went— Boston, New York, Baltimore, through the Midwest to Chicago and beyond—Halloween followed along. Irish Halloween rituals met with similar rituals practiced by blacks, Germans, English and Scots and gained momentum throughout the second half of the 19th century.

By the turn of the century, Halloween became a full-blown American holiday. The Victorians, always anxious to unearth quaint and historical entertainments, printed Halloween divination rituals in periodicals that finally reached a nationwide audience. Although the holiday was somewhat doctored to suit a Victorian readership, Halloween at last made its proper debut in American society.

By the 20th century, Halloween was gaining popularity with a national public. It survived its doggedly silly late Victorian incarnation; was employed as a tool to teach immigrants American history; and metamorphosed into a townwide family party on the scale of the Fourth of July celebration. Today, Halloween is an American treasure, celebrated in every corner of the country as the most bewitching night of inversion in our year.

A Blending
of Traditions _____ 1

On one autumn night each year, the fires of Druid priests burned high upon the Irish hillsides while Celtic tribesmen prayed that their sun would not wane and disappear over the winter. In Wales, each member of a family marked a white stone and threw it into the hot ashes of a bonfire before going to sleep; if any of the stones were missing by morning, they believed a death would surely occur before the next Halloween. Scottish farmers lit torches made of braided straw and marched *deosil* (with the sun) around the perimeters of their land to ward off witches and bring fertility to the fields. The Celts of Gaul imprisoned cats in wicker baskets and burned them in sacrificial fires. And in old Brittany, families put out warm pancakes and cider for dead souls to eat when they rose from their cold, barren graves to visit their homes before the coming of winter.

The history of Halloween traces a path from ancient Druidic times to the present. Originally a Celtic festival of the dead, Halloween owes much of its character to the Roman harvest celebration of the goddess Pomona and even more to the customs of the early Catholic church. It is the blending of these three traditions that produced the holiday we celebrate in America today.

The Celtic Festival of Samhain

Great was the darkness of that night,
and demons would appear on that night always.
　　　　　　　　—from *The Adventures of Nera*, an ancient Samhain tale

The history of Halloween begins in ancient times in the lands populated by Celtic peoples—what is now northern France, Ireland, England, Scotland, Wales and Brittany. Centuries before the birth of Christ, these rugged peoples forged a life-style from their hunting and herding. They celebrated two major seasonal events: the onset of winter, when the herds were brought in to shelter, and the onset of summer, when the herds could be released to pasture.

In the climate of northern Europe, winter came early—around November—and lasted close to six months. The first day of winter was considered the beginning of the new year, and celebrated as New Year's Day. Only the finest of the herd were brought to shelter on this day. The others were slaughtered, making it an occasion of great feasting and celebration. From the very beginning, this communal feast was dedicated to the Celtic Lord of the Dead (the festival opposite Samhain on the Celtic seasonal calendar, approximately May 1, was known as *Beltane* and heralded the grazing season).

The festival of Samhain was the most sacred of all Celtic festivals. Its rituals helped link people with their ancestors and the past. The Celts believed that the dead rose on the eve of Samhain and that ancestral ghosts and demons were set free to roam the earth, harm crops and trouble homes. Since spirits were believed to hold the secrets of the afterlife and the future, the priests of the Celts, the Druids, believed that on the eve of Samhain predictions had more power and omens could be read with more clarity. Druid priests divined the health of the tribe, the wisdom of a proposed move, the right time to make magic or the key to curing a sickness.

The Druids were also closely linked to witchcraft. For practitioners of this ancient craft, the festival of Samhain was one of their major annual celebrations, which may explain why witches are bound to Halloween

*The Celtic World was overrun
with spirits, demons and magic.
Here, a rendering of a medieval
witch suggests the themes of Halloween in our own time—bats,
flames and a pitch black night.
(From the frontispiece: Richard
Boulton,* The Possibility and
Reality of Magick, Sorcery,
and Witchcraft Demonstrated,
*Roberts, London, 1722; courtesy
of the Henry Lea Library, Dept.
of Special Collections, Van
Pelt Library, University of
Pennsylvania)*

imagery even today (in fact, Samhain remains a principal sabbath among modern day-witches and other neo-Pagans).

Samhain marked the start of the season that rightly belonged to evil spirits—a time when nights were long, and dark fell early. It was a frightening time for a people who were entirely subject to the forces of nature, and who were superstitious about the unknown, with only a primitive sympathetic magic system to rely on for comfort. Samhain was a night of mystical glory.

> ...the night of its eve was the great occasion in the year when the temporal world was thought to be overrun by the forces of magic. Magical troops issued from caves and mounds, individual men might even be received into these realms; whilst against the royal strongholds, assaults by flame and poison were attempted by monsters.[1]

Each year on Samhain, the Lord of the Dead was believed to assemble all lost souls for resentencing. This was the "Samhain Vigil," held during the darkest part of the night. Samhain judged the dead, sentencing sinning souls to 12 months of afterlife spent in the shape of a lowly animal. Good souls were sentenced to another 12 months of death, but were allowed to take the shape of human beings.

The Celts believed that gifts could make the Lord more temperate on this night, and offerings were made in hopes that he would allow the spirits of their loved ones a brief visit home to enjoy a warm fire and the smell of good food cooking. Food and wine were set out for the dead souls of the ancestors, sure to be weary from their travels in the netherworld. To avert unwanted guests—those malicious spirits set free on that night—the Celts hid themselves in ghoulish disguise so that the spirits wandering about would mistake them for one of their own and pass by without incident. Masked villagers representing the souls of the dead also attempted to trick the spirits by forming a parade and leading them to the town limits. If they thought appeasement or gentle persuasion was more appropriate, the Celts offered sweets to the spirits.

Because the festival of Samhain was a community gathering, and because it was the first of the new year, it was also the day to take care of annual business. People paid debts, renewed rents and land tenures, and bought and sold livestock and land.

A 20th-century Samhain made its animated debut in Walt Disney's 1940 feature film classic, Fantasia. *Here the supreme lord of evil, Chernabog, summons up the spirits of the dead on Walpurgis Nacht. (Cortlandt Hull Collection; © 1940 Walt Disney Productions.)*

The Festival of Taman

The Celtic New Year was also the time to celebrate the life-giving sun god, Baal. People believed that the sun grew weaker during the winter months, and feared it would leave them forever in the cold night of winter. The Celts celebrated a second feast, known as Taman, on November 1 to please and glorify the sun so that it would not disappear during the long, cold months ahead. Since they believed that like begets like, a bonfire was lit high on a hill—and still is in parts of Scotland and Wales—in an attempt to fuel the waning sun. Each member of the village could take part in this renewing ritual by rekindling their home fires from a "new fire" built on the last day of October.

Horses, believed sacred to the sun god, were sacrificed in great fires, and the Druids divined the future by observing the movements and entrails of the animals as they died. Evidence suggests that the Druids also sacrificed humans during these festivals. They imprisoned criminals— possibly practitioners of black magic—in wicker cages built to resemble animals and burned them. There were incidences of sacrificing horses to the sun as late as A.D. 400. And even in the Middle Ages, cats were burned in wicker cages on the November 1st fires.[2]

Taman and Samhain rituals were a vital part of Celtic culture; their secrets were passed from generation to generation through the oral tradition of the Druid priests. The kernels of many of America's Halloween traditions can be found in these ancient celebrations; ghoulish masquerade parades, divination, fire and spirit magic are elements associated with Halloween to this day.

Other elements, such as romance and apple lore, came from another part of the world entirely. Just before the birth of Christ, the Celtic lands were conquered by legions of Roman soldiers, and the Druid Samhain practices merged with Roman mythological beliefs.

The Roman Festival of Pomona

To the Romans, the apple was a symbol of love and fertility. The Roman divinity Pomorum, or Pomona, was the goddess of orchards and the harvest. She was celebrated on November 1 with feasts featuring apples, nuts, grapes and other orchard fruits. According to Ovid's *Metamorphoses*:

Pomona lived, when Procas, next in line,
Reigned o'er the people of the Palatine.
She tended orchards, and in care of trees
Was first among the woodland deities.
No Latian rival could surpass her pride
In fruit-tree culture—as her name implied.
She loved not woods and streams, but garden-ground,
Where laden boughs with smiling fruits abound.[3]

Pomona was a nymph who delighted in pruning and grafting, but would have nothing to do with men. She was beloved of several rustic divinities: Silvanus, Picus, but especially Vertumnus. Vertumnus was god of the "turning year", that is, of the seasons, and like Pomona, was especially important at harvest time. The youthful Vertumnus was able to change shape easily and disguised himself as anything from a visiting herdsman to a vine trimmer in order to catch sight of Pomona at work. One day he dressed as an old woman and was able to visit her long enough to speak this "prophecy":

How lovely the vine and the grapes are together,
and how different they would be apart, the tree
useless and the vine flat on the ground unable to
bear fruit. Are not you like such a vine? You turn
from all who desire you. You will try to stand alone.

And yet there is one—listen to an old woman who loves
you more than you know—you would do well not to reject
Vertumnus. You are his first love and his last. And he, too,
cares for the orchard and the garden. He could work by your side.[4]

Vertumnus then revealed himself to Pomona, who fell in love with him immediately. Forever after they tended the orchards together.

The festival of Pomona was celebrated on November 1, after the harvest was safely stored away for winter. It coincided with the Celt's Samhain festivities, and a synthesis naturally occurred. By the first century A.D., Romans and Celts inhabited the same scattered villages throughout Europe and most of the British Isles. Their life-styles merged and the pure origins of each culture's festivals were obscured.

The Roman celebration of the orchard harvest contributed the bounty of apples and nuts that remains a part of Halloween to this day. In the

British Isles of old, Samhain was sometimes called *Lamasabhal* ("Lamswool"), after a strong concoction of apples, sugar and ale that was drunk on the eve of November 1. The Druid belief that the eve of Samhain was the most potent night for prognostication seems also to have merged with aspects of the festival of Pomona: there are dozens of Halloween divination games from England, Ireland and Scotland that use apples and nuts to predict one's future spouse.

The Celtic and Roman cultures created what we might identify as Halloween in its ancient form. It was a night devoted to the dead, yet a night for divination and romance as well. But with the dawn of the first century A.D., an even greater marriage of traditions occurred. These pagan traditions came face to face with the new religion of Christianity.

All Saints' Day and All Souls' Day

You lie abed, and take your ease!
The poor Souls do so, never more!
You spread your limbs, and are at peace;
The Souls move from door to door.

Five boards, and one white sheet they have,
A wisp of straw beneath the head,
Five foot of earth to fill the grave
These are the riches of the dead![5]

Christianity spread across the Roman Empire and beyond from the first through the fourth centuries. The emperor Constantine officially declared Christianity legal and thousands of pagans were baptized into this new religion. The Church expounded a potent theology based on a holy trinity of one God, His Son, and the Holy Spirit. The pantheistic, nature-bound realm of Roman mythology was superseded. And although the new church decried the pagan practices of its enemies, it was in fact largely responsible for the health of pagan Halloween in Celtic countries. Rather than obliterate pagan ways, shrewd church leaders set about assimilating existing pagan rites into their new Christian ones.

Pagan folk had always celebrated a night when the dead returned; they had danced for centuries in the eerie light of the great fires on the eve of the festival of Samhain. The early Christians, as many scholars and folklorists suggest, were wise to let these rituals persist. Pope Gregory I declared: "Let the shrines of idols by no means be destroyed. Let water be consecrated and sprinkled in the temples, let altars be erected...so that the people, not seeing their temples destroyed, may displace error and recognize and adore the true God...And because they were wont to sacrifice to devils, some celebration should be given in exchange for this...they should celebrate a religious feast and worship God by their feasting, so that still keeping outward pleasure, they may more readily receive spiritual joys."[6]

The Church was looking to replace Samhain in the imaginations of their new converts, and although it took many years to make the transition, Samhain celebrations were gradually assimilated into the feasts of All Saints and All Souls.

The celebration of All Saints' Day is attributed to Pope Boniface IV, who dedicated the Roman temple, the Pantheon, to St. Mary and the Martyrs on the 13th of May, 610. Boniface set the day aside as a memorial to early Christians who died for their beliefs without official recognition of their sanctity, so that "the memory of all the saints might in future be honored in the place which had formerly been devoted to the worship, not of gods, but of demons."[7]

In the eighth century, Pope Gregory III re-established this festival on November 1 to honor the saints of St. Peter's Church. That the date coincided with Samhain was no accident: the Church was still trying to absorb the pagan celebrations taking place at this time. Later, Pope Gregory IV extended the festival to embrace all saints so that its celebration would reach every church under Roman rule (all churches had patron saints).

The clergy encouraged their flock to remember the dead with prayers instead of sacrifices. People were taught to bake "soul cakes"—little pastries and breads—to offer in exchange for blessings rather than trying to appease the spirits with food and wine. Soul cakes were given to the town's poor; in return, the poor would pray for departed family members. (The custom was initially a charitable one and ensured that the town's indigent would have something to eat at Hallowmas. Over time, the custom would grow more popular, and young men and boys would go from house to house singing "souling" songs, but asking for ale, food or money instead of soul cakes.)

Villagers were also encouraged to masquerade on this day, not to frighten unwelcome spirits, but to honor Christian saints. On All Saints' Day, churches throughout Europe and the British Isles displayed

A HALLOWMAS SOUL CAKE SONG

Soul day, Soul day,
We be come a-souling.
Pray good people remember the poor,
And give us a soul cake.
One for Peter, two for Paul,
Three for Him that made us all
An apple, a pear, a plum or a cherry
Or any good thing to make us merry.

Soul day, Soul day,
We have been praying for the soul departed.
So pray good people give us a cake
For we are all poor people,
Well known to you before.
So give us a cake for charity's sake,
And our blessing we'll leave at your door.

—from Poole, Customs, Superstitions, and
Legends of Staffordshire, *quoted from the*
English publication Bilston Mercury.
(English Folk-Rhymes *by G. F. Northall,*
Kegan Paul, Trench, Tribner & Co.,
reissued by Singing Tree Press, Detroit,
1968.)

relics of their patron saints. Poor churches could not afford genuine relics and instead had processions in which parishioners dressed as saints, angels and devils. This religious masquerade resembled the pagan custom of parading ghosts to the town limits. It served the new church by giving an acceptable Christian basis to the custom of dressing up on Halloween.

In addition, the Church tried to convince the people that the great bonfires they lit in homage to the sun would instead keep the devil away—God's mortal enemy in the new Christian religion.

All Souls' Day had its origins in the early ninth century, as a special commemoration of the dead declared by Amalarius in his *De Ordine antiphonarii*: "After the office of the saints I have inserted the office for the dead."[8]

In A.D. 993 the Benedictine abbot Saint Odilo of Cluny formally requested that All Souls' Day be placed in the books of the Church, basing his request on a directive he'd found in the scriptures of the Apocrypha:

> And the noble Judas exhorted the people to keep themselves free from sin, after having seen with their own eyes what had happened because of the sin of those who had fallen. He also took a collection, amounting to two thousand silver drachmas, each man contributing, and sent it to Jerusalem, to provide a sin offering, acting very finely and properly in taking account of the resurrections. For if he had not expected that those who had fallen would rise again, it would have been superfluous and foolish to pray for the dead; or if it was through regard for the splendid reward destined for those who fall asleep in godliness, it was a holy and pious thought. *Therefore he made atonement for the dead, so that they might be set free from their sin.*
>
> —2 Maccabees, xii, 46

This is church history; the folk version of the origin of All Souls' Day is a different story altogether. According to legend, a pilgrim returning from the Holy Land was shipwrecked on an island. He met a hermit, who claimed he had heard the groans of tormented souls coming from a huge flaming gorge. The pilgrim made his way to Cluny, told the abbot Odilo, and the abbot appointed November 2 as a day to pray for these souls.[9]

Since All Saints' Day had been widely celebrated on November 1, Abbot Odilo chose November 2 to be observed as a feast for all the departed. The date was chosen to follow All Saints' Day to reinforce the notion of a "communion of saints" and perhaps to reassure grieving relatives that their lost loved ones were in good company. The feast day was approved by Pope Sylvester II around A.D. 1000, and the observance of November 2 as All Souls' Day spread throughout Europe from the 11th through the 14th centuries.

The early Church's contribution to the popular celebration of Halloween was a considerable one. The Church ironically gave the holiday its name—during medieval times All Saints' Day was known as All Hallows, making the night before it All Hallows Eve, which became Hallowe'en, then Halloween. The Church sanctioned the long-standing custom of remembering the dead on the eve of November 1. Furthermore, it added credence to the old Celtic masquerades, parades and great blazing fires set on the dark evening before November 1. It was the Church, too, that firmly established the custom of visiting from house to house on All Hallows Eve—a practice that eventually evolved into America's most popular contemporary Halloween custom: trick or treating.

The Church brought its saints' celebrations to every new land it conquered. The celebrations on the eve of All Saints, All Saints' Day and All Souls' Day (the three were referred to as Hallowmas) spread throughout Europe. From the British Isles to France to Poland and Italy, the religious remembrance of the ancestral dead became an annual celebration of major importance. Each celebration retained a bit of its pagan mystery and each picked up the nuances of its host country.

In the British Isles during a medieval Halloween, a lonely bell ringer walked the narrow cobbled streets of tiny villages to warn that ghosts were on their way. Carved-out, candle-lit turnips sat on gateposts to ward off evil spirits, while people swore they heard the devil playing music with castanets made from dead men's bones. Hearth fires were lit and soul cakes were baked and stacked by the door. The town's poor came begging, offering prayers for the dead in return for a soul cake.

In Spain, a special pastry called "bones of the holy" was given away, and in Brittany people poured milk over the graves to feed the dead. In Salerno, Italy, families prepared huge banquets, set them out on a table in their homes and left for church. If the food wasn't gone when they returned, it was a very bad omen, meaning the dead disdained the food and the hospitality offered.

ALL SOULS' BREAD RECIPE

8 cups flour	1 tsp. grated orange rind
2 cups milk	1 tsp. grated lemon rind
4 yeast cakes	½ cup butter
8 egg yolks	1 tsp. salt
2 cups suger	

Dissolve yeast in ½ cup milk. Mix yeast with milk and one cup flour. Sprinkle top with flour and let rise. Add salt, egg yolks, beat until thick. Add sugar and rinds and mix with other ingredients. Add 2 cups flour, alternating with milk, and knead for ½ hour. Add remaining flour and butter and knead until dough comes away from hands. Set dough in a warm place until it rises to double in bulk. Separate into 4 parts, braid. Brush top with beaten egg yolks and sprinkle with poppy seed. Let rise. Bake at 350° for one hour.

—*Francis X. Weiser, Weston College, Weston, Massachusetts* (*from* The Holyday Book, *Harcourt, 1956*)

Polish Catholics taught their children to pray out loud as they walked through the woods so that the souls of the dead could hear them and be comforted. Priests in tiny Spanish villages still ring their church bells to remind parishioners to honor the dead on All Hallows Eve. And families throughout Catholic Europe visit village cemeteries with lit candles and gifts each Hallowmas. The Italians—a people with one of the most spirited relationships with their dead—even leave calling cards on the tombs of their dead relations.

Later on, these celebrations would figure largely in the picture of Halloween in America, as European immigrants flooded the young country in the 18th and 19th centuries. For now, our path leads us back to the British Isles, to pick up the threads of All Hallows as it existed prior to the first major immigration to wilderness America.

The Reformation and Guy Fawkes Day

It was on Halloween—October 31, 1517—that Martin Luther initiated a religious reformation that was to put a halt to the observance of Halloween for many Europeans. Influential theologians, such as Luther in Germany and the Frenchman John Calvin in Geneva, convincingly put forth a new concept of man's relationship with God. They said man worshiped with faith and good deeds rather than through the "icons," or symbols, of the Catholic church. They rejected the authority of the pope and looked exclusively to the Bible for guidance.

The individual man-to-God relationship struck a chord with many, and new Protestant sects formed throughout western Europe. Lutherans and Calvinists were pitted against Catholics in over 200 years of bitter battles. The Reformation eventually established freedom of dissent, but the price was dearly paid with lives and political tyranny.

Among the practices of the Catholic church to be abandoned by Reformation Protestants was the observance of saints' days. And without All Hallows' Day on the Protestant church calendar, there was of course no All Hallows' Eve.

But again, tradition would die hard. Much as Celtic Samhain was wed with the Roman festival of Pomona and much as these pagan feasts merged with Catholic custom, the English Protestants preserved an annual autumn fete in their secular rites. It was known as Guy Fawkes Day.

Please to remember
the fifth of November
Gunpowder, treason
and plot
I see no reason
Why Gunpowder treason
Should ever be forgot!
—Guy Fawkes Day song lyrics, sung in the 17th and 18th centuries

The anniversary of the gunpowder plot, better known as Guy Fawkes Day, dates from the heyday of Protestant-Catholic enmity in England. Fanatical Catholic leaders Robert Catesby and Thomas Winter (with the help of fellow Catholic revolutionary Guy Fawkes) devised a plot to blow up the Protestant-sympathetic House of Lords when Parliament met on November 5, 1605. The plan was foiled at the last minute, and Fawkes was captured as he entered the building's cellar to set his storehouse of gunpowder on fire. Fawkes was immediately arrested and later executed; the other conspirators soon met similar fates. Parliament passed an act in January 1606 declaring November 5 a day of national thanksgiving—a celebration of the triumph of Protestants over Catholics. Although people in Scotland, Ireland, Wales and some parts of western and northern England continued to celebrate Halloween in the late autumn, many English men and women eschewed it for Guy Fawkes Day.

The proximity of the celebrations—Guy Fawkes Day followed All Hallows' Eve by only by only six days—allowed for a great borrowing of traditions. Guy Fawkes Day was marked with great bonfires, and celebrants carried lanterns of hollowed-out turnips that had been fashioned into grotesque faces. The eve of Guy Fawkes Day became "mischief night" across most of northern England, an occasion for pranks and skylarking. Where once they had begged for "soul cakes" in commemoration of All Saints' Day, boys now dressed in costume and begged for lumps of coal to burn their effigies of Guy Fawkes. By the time King George III took the throne, just 15 years before the onset of the American Revolution, children had combined the Catholic soul-cake song with the Protestant coal-begging song:

Soul! Soul! for a lump of coal
A stick and a stake for King George's sake
Please to give a lump.

In the strongest Protestant regions of England, effigies of the pope were burned along with those of Guy Fawkes, and the holiday was known as Pope's Night. (Other luminaries enjoyed the same privilege over history: effigies of the Old Pretender, Napoleon, Cardinal Weisman, Nan Sahib, Kaiser Wilhelm II and Colonel Nasser were also burned in England.) In Lewes, where 17 Protestant martyrs were burned at the stake, children were more likely to sing

A rope, a rope, to hang the Pope
A piece of cheese to toast him,
A barrel of beer to drink his health,
And a right good fire to roast him.

Indeed, the fireworks, fires, masquerades, politics, pumpkins and pranks of Guy Fawkes Day were very much a part of the English fabric at the time of American colonization.

* * *

In days of old, people worshiped a Lord of the Dead because it helped them visualize the afterlife. Although the advent of Christianity brought about a new understanding of God, heaven and hell, people still needed to commune with their dead. The Church provided a Christian course of worship, and throughout medieval times people celebrated a half-pagan, half-Catholic All Hallows' Eve with fires, games, prayers, divinations, soul cakes and superstitious tales of the spirit world. Even in 17th-century England, revolutionary Protestants "borrowed" the bonfires, masquerades and itinerant mischief of All Hallows for their celebration of Guy Fawkes Day. By virtue of its being so adaptable to people's constantly changing needs, the holiday born on the dark night of October 31 has managed to survive nearly 2,000 years.

At the dawn of American colonization, Halloween traditions existed in several forms: in the All Hallows' celebrations of the Catholic church throughout Europe; in the old pagan folk customs of the British Isles; and in the secular Guy Fawkes Day festivities of the English Protestants. These were the elements of Halloween that the earliest settlers brought with them to the new world.

Notes

1. T.G.E. Powell, *The Celts*, Thomas Hudson, London and New York, 1958 and 1980, p. 147.
2. Sir James George Frazer, *The Golden Bough*, Volume I, abridged edition, Macmillan Publishing Co., New York, 1922, p. 761.
3. A. E. Watts, translator, *The Metamorphoses of Ovid, An English Version*, University of California Press, Berkeley, California, 1954, p. 337.
4. Edith Hamilton, *Mythology*, New American Library, New York, 1968, p. 286.
5. Anatole LeBraz, "All Souls' Eve in Lower Brittany," translated from the French for *The Living Age*, No. 2745, The Living Age Company, Boston, February 13, 1897.
6. John Greenway, *Folklore of the Great West*, American West Publishing Co., Palo Alto, California, 1970, p. 384.
7. Herbert Thurston and Donald Attwater, editors, *Butler's Lives of the Saints*, Volume IV, P.J. Kennedy and Sons, New York, 1956, pp. 234-235.
8. Ibid., p. 241.
9. Ebenezer Cobham Brewer, *Dictionary of Phrase and Fable*, Harper and Row Publishers, New York, 1959 and 1963, p. 23.

Forerunners to Halloween in the American Colonies _____ 2

Europeans in the 16th and 17th centuries heard tell of a great wilderness lying across the Atlantic to the west. Some eyed the New World as a stepping-stone to the gold and spices of Japan, China and the Indies beyond. Others hoped to find precious metals and natural resources. Farmers dreamed about acres and acres of fertile lands. America, they had heard, was populated by "noble savages"—primitive peoples living in an idyllic world plentiful with game.

The Spanish sent the first expeditions to Florida, New Mexico and southern California looking for gold. Then came the Dutch and English, settling in the east to mine the sea and trade the resources they found in America—wood, pitch, tar, corn and, eventually, tobacco—for European goods. The French ran the interior riverways, trading furs with Native Americans. Later, Germans and Scottish-Irish found farming land in the hills of Pennsylvania, and the Swedish found familiar terrain in the

The original caption to this Victorian drawing entitled "Halloween in Colonial Days" explains that the "whispering rod" was used by young people to communicate privately in the typically small Puritan home. This device is probably the product of the artist's fancy, as is the idea that Puritans would have celebrated a holiday called "Halloween." (Wuanita Smith, Harper's Weekly, *October 27, 1900, p. 1003.)*

midwest and north-central parts of the wilderness. This wave of settlement spanned the first 200 years of white history in America: by 1680, the European population of America was 200,000. It was a vast number considering the trek was made in tiny, often unseaworthy vessels. But the next 100 years would bring nearly 20 times that number to American shores.

During the 17th and 18th centuries, American colonization became an antidote for the social and financial ailments of Europe. The Agricultural Revolution provided new machinery that in effect displaced smaller farmers. These men and women looked to the New World for land. The Industrial Revolution had much the same effect on craftsmen. Factories took over the jobs they had performed for centuries and they came to America in droves to practice their trades. Added to this was the fact that advances in medicine, better living conditions and better food provided Europe with a surplus population. For many Europeans of modest means, emigration was a profitable alternative to joblessness. Lastly, religious differences and the emergence of Protestantism sent many thousand religious rebels to the New World in search of freedom of choice.

By the time of the first federal census in 1790, there were nearly 3,637,900 Europeans in the former colonies. They were predominantly British, yet as varied as all the nations of Europe—loosely organized bands of settlers with their own religions, histories and even separate languages. The existence of Hallowmas, or of any autumn holiday, depended entirely on the religious and folk fabric of each emerging colony. Whereas the Massachusetts Bay Colony, New Hampshire and Connecticut were populated by rigid Puritans and had a dearth of holidays, Rhode Island was settled in the spirit of religious freedom and encompassed many different life-styles. New York was colonized by the New Reformed Dutch, who brought with them a love for festivity. German and Swiss settlers became major influences in Pennsylvania, and their spiritual and folk traditions (particularly their magic and witchcraft traditions) figured largely in that colony. Maryland was settled by Catholics who brought along the Saints' days, symbols and feasts of the Old World, including Hallowmas. And Virginia was home to members of the Church of England—a church that celebrated the Catholic saints' days as well as some old English folk holidays. The beliefs of Spanish Catholics, African blacks and Anglicans all helped shape the folklife of the southern colonies and each contributed to Halloween traditions in the New World.

Some immigrant groups kept the religious remembrances of All Saints' and All Souls' Days, some the pagan intrigue with magic, witchcraft and the dead, and some the social aspects of romantic alliances and community gatherings. As wilderness America was peopled with new settlements, the colonies grew and evolved their own distinct autumn celebrations.

The Colony of Virginia

The English chapter in American history began in 1607 when three small ships set sail for the New World in hopes of finding abundant gold and a water course through the continent to the riches of China and Japan. Instead the 104 sea-weary adventurers peopled a settlement on the James River that would come to be known as Jamestown, Virginia.

Virginia grew to be the largest of the colonies, encompassing lands that included present-day Virginia, Wisconsin, Mississippi, Illinois, Indiana, Kentucky, Ohio, West Virginia and Minnesota. The colony came to be home not only to the English, but also to Germans, Poles, French, and Scots, as well as a large population of African blacks. But Virginia remained primarily English in her economic, social and religious life. As royal subjects, Virginians were typically of the Anglican faith.

The Anglican church developed from the Catholic church in the 16th century when Henry VIII came into conflict with Rome. Although Protestant, the Church of England kept the doctrine, liturgy and organization of the Roman Catholic church until Elizabeth I instituted her "middle way"—a compromise blending Protestant and Catholic elements. Although the adoration of saints' relics was condemned in this Anglican church, the celebration of saints' days was maintained.

Rest Eternal I grant unto them, O Lord,
And let light perpetual shine upon them.
May they rest in Peace.
Amen.

—Anglican prayer for All Saints' Day

The Anglican church calendar of 1662 lists All Souls' Day as an "unofficial holy day" and All Saints' Day as a first-class feast day.

Anglican church literature even allows for the "saying of vespers of the dead on All Saints' Day after Even song—or by itself at a later hour—as a popular observance,"[1] indicating that church members may have been observing a sort of private Halloween in accordance with folk tradition.

In addition to an official commemoration of the dead on All Saints' Day, the early colonial life of Virginia featured a lively folk belief in the spirit world and the occult. Settlers in trouble were often as likely to consult astrology, chiromancy (palmistry), fortune-telling or divination as they were their God. In doing so, they were simply continuing a tradition carried on by their cousins and parents in England.

Seventeenth-century Englishmen and women commonly consulted the world of magic for answers; numerous books were available and occult practitioners were frequently consulted, even by the educated upper classes. (English astrologer William Lilly, for example, had more than 2,000 occult consultations each year between 1645 and 1660.[2]) In the England the Virginian settlers left behind, Christian religion and occultism were not clearly separated into two distinct, nonintersecting spheres. As a result, early colonists accepted and practiced a good bit of magic, either in conjunction with their religion or independent of it. Occult practices existed everywhere in young America every one of the colonies had legal punishments for those convicted of using magic.[3] Witchcraft was the most publicized crime, but colonists were also tried for crimes of astrology, fortune-telling and "Magick Arts." The existence and knowledge of magic and divination were probably as crucial to the survival of modern Halloween as the health of All Saints' Day.

Books on alchemy, astrology, healing, German occultism, Hermeticism, herbal cures and the occult Rosicrucian movement appear in the historical library lists of colonial citizens. Early Virginia estate libraries commonly held a number of these books, such as the popular medical books by physician-astrologer Nicholas Culpeper. Edmund Berkeley, a Virginia Council member, owned the book *Physiognomy and Chiromancy*, and Virginia Anglican minister Thomas Teackle owned books on herbal magic, astrology, alchemy, Jewish mysticism and Christian Hermeticism. Almanacs including astrological data outsold the Bible in the colonies.[4]

The isolated, hardworking settlements that peopled the east coast in the 17th century were ideal for propagating the occult; the intimacy of a small, tightly knit village made it easy to pass on occult traditions and easier to accuse others of little sorceries and magic. According to historian Darrett

B. Rutman, an early Virginian could "…account his poor hunting to the spell of another (1626), could hold that only the horseshoe over his door protected his sick wife from the evil intentions of a neighbor woman who perforce passed under it on her way to saying black prayers at his wife's bedside (1671), could attribute to a witch the death of his pigs and withering of his cotton (1698)…"[5]

Witches, charms, futuring and spirits—some of Halloween's primary folk elements—were far from foreign to early Virginian settlers; neither were the communal elements of Halloween. The Anglicans were not opposed to enjoying their wealth, as were some of the other English Protestant sects who followed them to the New World. Drinking, dancing, gaming and racing were entertainments they considered well within the bounds of good taste and honest fun. Virginians carried on an old-world tradition of gathering together in the autumn to celebrate the harvest and encourage trade. Fairs were held in September and October in which horses, oxen, cows, sheep and hogs were sold and games and contests abounded. There were slow horse races, foot races, bag races or contests featuring a greased pig or goose. There were grinning contests, whistling contests, puppet shows, ropewalking and fortune-telling. These fairs were also used for paying debts, buying land and obtaining bills of exchange, just as in the old days of Samhain.

Early Virginians celebrated a joyous Christmas and feted the patron saint of England, Saint George, with dancing, singing, drinking and cavorting.[7] It is doubtful they let Guy Fawkes Day go by without proper celebration.

The American Guy Fawkes Day, also known as Powder Plot Day and Pope's Day, was celebrated with bonfires and boisterous public gatherings. Although the Anglicans were not vitriolic about the pope—their religion contained a healthy dose of Catholicism—their new neighbors certainly were. The Scottish Presbyterians, French Huguenots, German Lutherans and Quakers who came to Virginia were avidly anti-pope, and probably quietly approved of their English neighbors' spirited celebration of Powder Plot Day.

The seeds of American Halloween were planted in Virginia. The Anglican church's observance of Hallowmas maintained the official holiday, and the health of the magic arts in the colony ensured the practice of some of its folk elements. By the time of the Revolution, a boisterous American autumnal celebration of romance and the spirit world was beginning to take shape in the imagination of the people.

Massachusetts Bay Colony

Of the original New England colonies—New Hampshire, Massachusetts, Connecticut and Rhode Island—Massachusetts was the largest and most influential. It was settled by groups of English Calvinists known as Puritans, and the strength of their religious beliefs, folklore and morality remains a part of New England to this day.

Puritans were radical Protestants who rejected the compromise of Queen Elizabeth's "middle way." The Puritans thought the Church of England simply did not go far enough in exorcising Catholicism, and followed a strict Calvinist doctrine. Vocal, extreme and unpopular with non-Puritan English officials, a small number of these rebels made their way, via Leiden, Holland, to Plymouth Colony in the New World and established the first major Puritan settlement in America. After the ascension of Charles I—a Protestant king married to a Catholic queen and hence sympathetic to the pope—Puritan suppression in England grew unbearable. By 1634, 10,000 Puritans had immigrated to America.

Life in Massachusetts Bay Colony was demanding at best. Indian attacks came without warning and the harvests did not always yield enough to feed the colonists. To the self-appointed "saints" of Puritan New England, charged with God's mission to build a community dedicated to His service, festive holidays were but a faint, nostalgic memory. The colonists' day-to-day lives were filled with solemn prayer and public "thanksgivings" for the blessings of God—good harvests, ships come safely to port with supplies, survival through Indian attacks, the end of a sickness and the like.

In Puritan New England, only three holidays were officially celebrated: Muster Day (for showing off military skill and strength), Election Day, and the day of Harvard Commencement. Thanksgiving was the first official new holiday to appear, emerging in the 1630s and 1640s as a day of prayer followed by a large family dinner, set in the annual calendar to give thanks, regardless of what had happened in the previous 12 months.[8]

The saints' days of the Church of England were forbidden by law. Puritans had come to New England to escape religious persecution; anything remotely resembling Catholicism was scorned. But this absence of holidays left a void in Puritan folk life that was not completely filled with the passion of prayer, and there were some occasions where old secular traditions alleviated the bleakness of the social climate.

"THE GHOSTS"

The early colonists did not observe a "Day of the Dead" where ancestors returned and visited the living. But Indian tribes throughout most of America did celebrate such an occasion—usually at midsummer—and Henry Wadsworth Longfellow's poem "The Ghosts" (from "The Song of Hiawatha") describes Hiawatha's encounter with the dead:

> *Cries of grief and lamentation*
> *Reach us in the Blessed Islands;*
> *Cries of anguish from the living,*
> *Calling back their friends departed,*
> *Sadden us with useless sorrow.*
> *Therefore have we come to try you;*
> *No one knows us, no one heeds us.*
> *We are but a burden to you,*
> *And we see that the departed*
> *Have no place among the living.*

Halloween's "soul mate," May Day, seems to have enjoyed some observance in the early colonial period, as evidenced by Increase Mather's scathing attack on the day:

> It is an abominable shame that any persons in a land of such light and purity as New England has been, should have the face to speak or think of practicing so vile a piece of heathenism.[9]

In Quincy, Massachusetts, in 1628, there is a report of the Puritan militia suppressing a maypole celebration, complete with drinking and dancing. And a maypole was cut down in Charlestown, Massachusetts, as late as 1687.[10]

April Fools' Day survived in New England, although it was particularly disliked by the Puritan Judge Sewall:

> In the morning I dehorted Sam Hirst and Grindell Rawson from playing idle tricks because 'twas the first of April: They were the greatest fools that did so. N.E. men came hither to avoid anniversary days, the keeping of them such as 25th of Decr. How displeasing must it be to God the giver of our Time to keep anniversary days to play the fool with ourselves and others.[11]

Guy Fawkes Day was another story altogether. The people in England had enjoyed this day and the settlers weren't about to give it up. Even the first settlement at Plymouth saw a Guy Fawkes celebration, although it reputedly resulted in a massive fire in one of the public buildings.

Puritan church officials tried hard to rid their congregations of the holiday and its frivolity—they had already erased most other holidays from the calendar. But the people would have none of it, as an entry in Judge Sewall's diary attests:

> Mr. Allin preached, Nov. 5, 1685—finished his Text 1 Jn. I.9 mentioned not a word in Prayer or Preaching that I took notice of with respect to Gun-Powder Treason...Although it rained hard, yet there was a Bonfire made on the Comon, about 50 attended it. Friday night being fair, about two hundred hallowed about a fire on the Comon.

Masquerade and begging were frowned on as well by Puritan officials. In Governor Belcher's time (the first half of the 18th century), "the

AN ACCOUNT OF THE PURITAN MAY DAY
CELEBRATION AT MA-RE MOUNT

They also set up a May-pole, drinking and dancing about it many days together, inviting the Indian women, for their consorts, dancing and frisking together, (like so many faries, or furies rather) and worse practices. As they had anew revived and celebrated the feasts of the Roman Goddes Flora, or the beasly practieses of the Madd Bacchinalians. Morton likewise, (to shew his poetrie) composed sundry rimes and verses, some tending to lasciviousnes, and others to the detraction and scandall of some persons, which he affixed to this idle or idoll May polle.

—from the diary of William Bradford, 1628, as excerpted in Colonial Holidays, *Doubleday Page & Co., New York, 1910.*

May Day and Halloween originate from the same Celtic folk culture. Although scant and isolated Puritan celebrations of May Day are documented, it appears that Halloween was banished completely. (Boston Public Library Photo Collection)

stopping of pedestrians on the street by 'loose and dissolute' people, who were wont to levy contributions for paying for their bonfires, became so universally annoying that the governor made proclamation against them in the newspapers."[12] Still, in tiny villages throughout New England, parades of young man and boys dressed in fantastic costume and carried "Guys" or "popes" of straw.

As the young nation grew and the strictness of the Puritan leaders relaxed, Pope's Day was publicly known as an evening for rejoicing and drink:

> Spent the evening at Mr. Pynchon's, with Farnham, Sewall, Sargeant, Col. Saltonstall & ct. very agreeably. Punch, wine, bread and cheeses, apples, pipes, tobacco and Popes and bonfires this evening at Salem, and a swarm of tumultuous people attending.
> —John Adams, in Salem court records for November 5, 1766

Guy Fawkes Day celebrations also retained their political potency. In the pre-revolutionary celebrations of New England, the Stamp Man—an effigy representing the unpopular stamp tax—was burned alongside the pope and the Devil.

The holiday gradually receded in importance as the colonies developed their own history, heroes and villains, until celebrations appeared only in isolated New England villages. Frederick D. Allen writes in his *Dialect Notes*: "...the observances have dwindled to hornblowing, and the carrying about of pumpkin lanterns by the boys. The origin of the celebration is quite forgotten."[13] The masked begging then became part of the Thanksgiving holiday, and a disdainful description deplored the "importune begging on Thanksgiving Day of ragged fantastics, usually children of Roman Catholic parents."[14] Guy Fawkes Day celebrations eventually disappeared during the American Revolution, in which the Catholic French aided the patriots; the Pope's Day celebrations may have been an embarrassment. The holiday was abolished in the States in 1833.

As for Halloween in the New England colonies, there was no mention of it whatsoever. There could be no greater anathema to the Puritans than a pagan celebration of the spirit world. Ritual celebration and Catholic theology were seen as manifestations of an unfathomable evil, and the Puritans could not reconcile these beliefs with their own God. More than that, Halloween was born of a respect for the ancestral dead and the past. Puritan New England was too new for ancestors, and the Puritans had precious little respect for the past. The Puritans did, however, take a passionate interest in the spirit world—an interest that manifested itself in a fearful fascination with witchcraft and divination.

The Puritans brought a fully developed fear of witchcraft and a long tradition of persecuting witches to the colonies. Because witches are so inextricably woven into the fabric of old Halloween in Europe and contemporary Halloween in America, it is worth examining the Puritans' understanding of "the craft."

Witchcraft is essentially a religion based on beliefs that form a strong, interactive relationship between the witch and the natural world.[15] Witches were familiar with herbal medicines and "potions," and knowledgeable about planting seasons, weather, breeding patterns and other vital aspects of rustic life. Some believe that the religion was strong enough in the Middle Ages to form a viable threat to the Catholic church. In the 1300s, the *Malleus Maleficarum* ("Witches' Hammer") was published by inquisitors Heinrich Institor and Jakob Sprenger as the first printed encyclopedia of demonology. The document had a devastating effect: it created a link between witchcraft and the Devil, and cast witches as the enemy of the Christian church. Witchcraft predates the concept of the Christian devil by centuries, but the Church produced a mythology so potent that witchcraft has been associated with evil to this day. The fearsome imaginations of these 14th-century popes and priests were ultimately responsible for the horrifying descriptions of witches' magic our Puritan ancestors drummed up during the witch trials in America. The most famous incidence of witch hysteria took place less than 30 miles outside of Boston, the hub of the Massachusetts Bay Colony.

By the late 1690s, the fear and superstition, struggle and frustration that were such a large part of Puritan life for many long years came to a head. In the small congregation of Salem Village (now Danvers, Massachusetts), a group of adolescent girls began having bizarre fits and creative "possessions," allegedly the work of local women they identified as witches. The possessions took the community by surprise. The Puritan judges looked quickly to England for protocol; England herself had been through a revival of witch-hunting in 1645, and courts there had established admissible evidence and legal procedures for convicting witches.[16] The Salem courts tried scores of citizens from every walk of life for the crime of witchcraft. By the time the hysteria had run its course, 20 people were dead, hanged or pressed to death for refusing to confess to crimes they had not committed.

The average Puritan propagated his own fear and imagined witches where there were none. Some, seizing on the opportunity, blamed witch-

WITCHCRAFT AND THE LAW

*In 1603, King James' Parliament enacted a law outlining the evidence
necessary for witchcraft conviction and sentencing. As the Puritan courts
in America had no experience of their own regarding witchcraft, they
looked to laws such as this one for guidance in the trials of 1692:*

> *If any person shall use any invocation or conjuration of any evil or
> wicked spirit; or shall consult, covenant with, entertain, employ,
> feed or reward any evil or cursed spirit to or for any intent or
> purpose; or take up with any dead man, woman, or child out of the
> grave, or the skin, bone, or any part of the dead person, to be
> employed or used in any manner of witchcraft, sorcery, charm or
> enchantment, or shall use, practice or exercise any sort of witch-
> craft, sorcery, charm or enchantment; whereby any person shall be
> destroyed, killed, wasted, consumed, pined or lamed in any part of
> the body; that every such person, being convicted, shall suffer
> death.*

—from George William Douglas, The American Book of Days,
*revised by Helen Douglas Compton, H.W. Wilson Company,
New York, 1948, p. 567.*

craft for misdeeds such as thievery and for sickness. Others conveniently used the charge of witchcraft to rid the community of misfits or to seize land or property they found useful.[16]

To the most educated of the Puritans, the witch was an outward manifestation of God's anger and the Devil's power. To the colonial farmer and shopkeeper, the witch was a domestic threat, interfering with butter or milk, livestock or marriage. In either case, witches were not thought to have any connection with Halloween in young America; they were assumed to fly to all-night frolics just about any night of the year. It would be a good 200 years before the general public once more associated witchcraft with the night of October 31.

Massachusetts Puritans rejected the symbolism of the Catholic church, but when it came to the spirit world symbolism ignited their imaginations. This 17th-century account of a haunting includes a battery of old-world symbols cloaked in a "realistic and true" account of some peculiar happenings:

> In the house of William Morse of Newbury, in 1679, an invisible hand hurled bricks, sticks, and stones, about; threw a cat at the woman of the house; caused a long staff to dance up and down the chimney and resist the efforts of two persons to place it on the fire; whirled an iron crook about; tossed a chair on the dining table in the midst of the meat; scattered ashes over the suppers, heads and clothes of the family, beat a bag of hops taken from a chest; hit the man of the house with several instruments, one being a besom [broom], while he was at prayer; and threw foul corn in with the clean while the people were winnowing.[18]

It is interesting to see the work of what would have been called fairies in England, and the references to a cat and a broom (old witch associations). More interesting is the account of ashes scattered over the family, like some Catholic ritual perverted, and the man being disturbed at prayer. It seems that Puritan ghost stories, especially those told by theologians, often had a moral lesson neatly built in for the listener. They also helped keep the spirit imagery of the Old World alive in the imaginations of their people.

There is a considerable body of religious history and literature about the Puritans in New England—enough to give the impression that all the men, women and children in the colonies there were devout, pious churchgoers. In truth, only one-third of adults in New England belonged to a church after 1650, and New England was relatively populous. (In the middle colonies and the south, the percentage was much less.[19]) Like their fellow colonists to the south in Virginia, New Englanders relied on magic as well as religion for help in their daily lives.

The blending of the occult into religion was something well known to early colonists and their English ancestors. This synthesis, as religious historian Jon Butler suggests, seems reasonable based on the philosophical similarity between Calvinism and the occult:

> The fatalism inherent in Calvinism's concept of predestination found an occult equivalent in the idea fundamental to astrology that motions of stars and planets revealed a future that individuals could not control. Calvinist evangelists and occult practitioners also explained catastrophes in similar ways. Believers in occult ideas thought the coming of comets and eclipses had inescapable and usually disastrous consequences; not even kings and queens escaped their verdicts. No one escaped judgement by the Calvinist God either.[20]

In Puritan New England, fortune-telling games were very popular. For most young girls, marriage and homemaking offered the only escape from their parents' homes; who and when to marry were of paramount importance. Although the Puritan religious leaders naturally condemned fortune-telling as heresy, adolescent girls were girls first and Puritans second. An obsession with divination was one of the main reasons Salem's young girls were drawn to the vodoun of the black-Indian slave Tituba; certainly divination was one of the "black arts" they were practicing when young Betty Parris accused her first witch and set Salem hysteria in motion. As Marion Starkey states in *The Devil in Massachusetts*: "...the girls were in and out of the Parris household and learning much from Tituba. Probably what they were chiefly after was fortune-telling. Not only were they at the age when the future is full of unsounded mystery, but in New England at large many people old enough to known better were currently solacing their uncertainties by practicing what Cotton Mather called 'little sorceries,' by conjuring with sieve and scissors and candle."[21]

In the unique and feisty Massachusetts community of Marblehead, unmarried women customarily hung a pot of tallows over the fire, then dropped iron hobnails into the fat, believing their husbands-to-be would appear during the process.[22] This divination resembles the old Celtic Halloween custom of dropping hot lead into water to reveal the status of

The elderly and ailing Rebecca Nurse was one of the saddest casualties of the strong Puritan belief in a hostile spirit world. Convicted of witchcraft by the Salem court, she was hanged on July 19, 1692. She professed her innocence to the last. Her graveside monument reads:

O Christian Martyr who for Truth could die
When all about thee owned the hideous lie!
The world, redeemed from superstition's sway
Is breathing freer for thy sake to-day

one's future mate (if the lead shape resembled a ship, he would be a sailor; a coffin meant widowhood). Marblehead girls also threw balls of yarn from upper windows onto the streets for their future husbands to pick up.[23] This was the exact ritual practiced by girls in the British Isles on Halloween for centuries.

New Hampshire

The colony of New Hampshire was a dissenting offshoot of Massachusetts Bay Colony. Although early New Hampshire settlers warred continually with Massachusetts about land and independence, many aspects of life in the tiny colony resembled those of Puritan Massachusetts (the two colonies even shared one governor for 42 years).

Guy Fawkes Day, for instance, was as cherished by New Hampshire settlers as it was in Massachusetts. In Anglican-influenced Portsmouth, Guy Fawkes Day celebrations had gotten so rowdy that they were forbidden in 1768 by official order of the colonial assembly.[24] In Newcastle, New Hampshire, the holiday was called Pork Night and was observed with great gusto, fires and pranks. New Hampshire colonials also celebrated the bounty of salmon and shad, and corn, apples and maple sugar in annual fall harvest festivals. These were occasions for the whole community to come together for drinking and games—not unlike the European gatherings centered around the apple and nut harvests.

Connecticut

Connecticut was initially settled by Dutch traders from New Netherland (later renamed New York), but as time went on attracted many more discontented Puritans from Massachusetts Bay Colony. Although the colony was founded because its leaders found the Massachusetts government too autocratic, Connecticut eventually developed a similarly rigid government. There was an assumed union of church and state, and the Connecticut church was Congregational—a church resembling Puritanism in doctrine. It is not surprising then, considering the great similarity, that the Connecticut colony made little apparent contribution to American Halloween tradition.

JOHNATHAN BUCK OF BUCKSPORT

The incidents surrounding the life of Johnathan Buck, founder of Bucksport, Maine, are a good example of the witch lore handed down from later Puritan times. This story gets told around Bucksport with renewed conviction each Halloween—no doubt enhancing its effect on the younger generation. It is a popular test of courage to visit Buck's grave on October 31.

Buck was a severe and Puritannical judge who once ordered the execution of a woman accused of witchcraft. The woman went to her death cursing Buck, who stood unmoved. At the moment of her death she allegedly shouted this prophecy:

"Johnathan Buck, listen to these words, the last my tongue will utter. It is the spirit of the one and only true and living God which bids me speak them to you. You will soon die. Over your grave they will erect a stone, that all may known where your bones are crumbling into dust. But listen, upon that stone the imprint of my foot will appear, and for all time, long after you and your accursed race has perished from this earth, will the people from far and near know that you murdered a woman."

—quoted in Haverhill *(Mass.)* Gazette, *March 22, 1899, as cited in* Johnathan Buck of Bucksport *by Blakely B. Babcock (*Ellsworth American Press, *Ellsworth, Maine, 1981.)*

Townspeople say Buck probably never judged this nameless woman and the Bucksport, Maine, librarian reports there were never any witch trials as far north as Bucksport. But on the grave of Johnathan Buck, there is indeed a hazy black outline of a boot etched in the stone.

Like the other New England colonies, however, Connecticut celebrated autumn festivals with the harvesting of corn and apples. Sugaring celebrations, apple paring and cornhusking parties provided
entertainment and a sense of community that the settlers looked forward to each fall.

Connecticut, too, had its share of witch mythology. The popular English
"water test" was used to determine a witch's guilt in that colony: the
accused was usually bound and dunked in water—if she floated, she was
a witch, if she drowned, she was not. In 1692, in Fairfield, two accused
witches were "bound hand and foot and put into the water, and they swam
like cork, and one labored to press them into the water, and they buoyed
up like cork."[25]

Rhode Island

Roger Williams was a Puritan minister serving in Salem in 1633. He
angered other colonials with his views on the separation of church and
state, professing the belief that magistrates could not punish breaches of
religious laws, only moral and civil ones. He was banished from Massachusetts and established Providence, Rhode Island, in 1636. Breaking
with tradition completely, Williams formed no official church in his
colony, but cultivated a spirit of religious tolerance. Under his gover-
nance, many disparate religions coexisted in Rhode Island: there was a
small Jewish community in Newport and the first Baptist church was
founded, with Williams' help, in Providence. There were Anglicans in
Narragansett and Newport who continued practicing old-world holidays
such as Christmas and Easter:

> On this anniversary [Easter] the people of the town crowded the
> beaches to see if the sun would "dance" as it came up; for if it
> "danced," the year was sure to be a lucky one for those who
> watched.[26]

America's first major Quaker settlement also established itself in
Rhode Island. The Society of Friends, or Quakers, did not celebrate
Hallowmas. Like the Puritans before them, they rejected anything popish
or Catholic. But, also like the Puritans before them, they acknowledged
a healthy spirit world; the link between miracles, cures and magic was one

many early American Quakers could make. It was essential to the acceptance of a physically present spirit world—the domain of Halloween.

Although Halloween celebrations were not a feature of colonial New England, New England did preserve some elements of the holiday. Fall harvest celebrations became commonplace as New Englanders set down roots and developed communities from their once isolated settlements and farms. The Puritans' acceptance of witch magic, ghost stories and divination paved the way for autumn get-togethers that would feature just these things. The lusty celebration of Guy Fawkes fulfilled the early colonists' need for a secular autumn holiday and allowed them to keep their ancient bonfires. Guy Fawkes pumpkins, masquerades and begging were safely stored on the 5th of November; years later, they would be used again on the last day of October.

The middle colonies had a different character altogether. Dutch traders influenced the early life of this region, along with English, German, Scottish and even Catholic settlers. The folk and occult life of this region was a lively one.

New York

The Dutch colony of New Netherland was founded with strict religious guidelines. Founding fathers were members of the Dutch Reformed church, a Calvinist religion hostile to practices such as celebrating All Saints' Day or venerating holy objects unless substantiated by Scripture. In its Charter of 1640, the colony declared, "No other religion shall be publicly admitted in New Netherland except the Reformed."

The colony passed from Dutch to English hands in 1664 and was given to the Duke of York. The Anglican church then became its official religion and by the late 17th century was established by law in four major New York counties. In the years that followed, several different religious groups settled there. King James II's conversion to Catholicism paved the way for many Catholics; however, when William and Mary ascended the throne, Catholics were again persecuted, and their presence diminished. French Huguenots found their way to the east coast of New York, and Mennonites from Pennsylvania settled the farmlands of western New York. Each new religious group brought with it an aspect of Halloween: the Catholic and Anglican churches kept active the observances of All Saints' Day at Hallowmas, and the German Mennonites brought a cultural history including the vivid occult practices of German peoples. The New York Dutch, by far the most influential in the folk customs and politics of the colony, brought an enthusiasm for holidays that had been absent from grim New England.

The Dutch in New York celebrated New Year's Eve as well as May Day, where they put up maypoles, got drunk and fired their guns. It was also customary to go visiting from house to house on New Year's, with bands of Dutchmen sharing ale and spirits at every stop. They also celebrated Shrovetide in great style, incurring a proclamation from Reformed Dutch Governor Peter Stuyvesant that stated that certain farmer's servants were "forbidden and interdicted...to ride the goose at the feast...of Shrovetide...because it is altogether unprofitable, unnecessary, and criminal for subjects and neighbors to celebrate such pagan and popish feasts and to practice such customs, not withstanding the same may be in some places of the Fatherland be tolerated and looked at through fingers."[27] ("Riding the goose" was a game played by hanging a greased goose between two poles; the object was to catch and hold on while the goose flew by.) The Dutch men sometimes masqueraded in women's clothes at Shrovetide, and paraded the streets to the delight of the town. This Shrovetide celebration was practiced by the Dutch in Philadelphia and Baltimore as well.[28]

Another holiday early New Yorkers brought with them from the fatherland was Guy Fawkes Day:

> Saturday last, being the fifth of November, it was observed here in Memory of that horrid and Treasonable Popish Gun-Powder Plot to blow up and destroy King, Lords and Commons, and the Gentlemen of his Majesty's Council; the Assembly and Corporation and other the principal Gentlemen and Merchants of this City waited upon his Honor the Lieutenant-Governor at Fort George, where the Royal Healths were drunk, as usual, under the discharge of the Cannon, and at the Night the city was illuminated.
> —*New York Gazette*, November 7, 1737[29]

In New York in 1775, an effigy of the governor was burned with the Devil in celebration of the Stamp Act Congress's declaration that the stamp tax was unconstitutional. Colonists carried torches, fired pistols and congregated around a raging bonfire to cheer the mock roasting of their political enemies.

Romantic colonials celebrated Saint Valentine's Day. In New York, women carried a heavy cord with a knotted end and hit every man they met.[30] Colonial customs regarding saints' days were often laced with this sort of folk tradition, as evidenced by this description of a Valentine's Day custom practiced in New York in 1754:

> Last Friday was St. Valentine's Day, and the night before I got five bay leaves and pinned four on the corners of my pillow, and the fifth in the middle; and then if I dreamt of my sweetheart, Betty said we should be married before the year was out. But to make it more sure I boiled an egg and took out the yolk and filled it with salt; and when I went to bed ate it shell and all, without speaking or drinking after it. We also wrote our lover's names upon bits of paper, and rolled them up in clay and put them into water; and the first that rose up was to be our Valentine.[31]

Similar charms and divinations had been attached to Halloween for generations.

New Jersey

New Jersey had ties to New York, New England and Pennsylvania throughout much of its early history. The colony was settled by the Dutch, then given to the Duke of York much as New York had been. The Dutch and English eventually divided New Jersey in two—the east was given to Englishman George Carteret and populated by Dutch people from New York, Scots (imported to be servants), Anglicans, Baptists, and Congregationalists. New England Puritans settled in Newark and influenced the colony's northeastern section. Western New Jersey was given to the Quakers, and was similar to Pennsylvania in character. William Penn eventually bought Carteret's half to form one whole colony. In 1702, the Jerseys became a royal English colony.

The early cultural influences on eastern New Jersey are similar to New York's. The Dutch and English made significant contributions to that colony's secular and religious celebrations. Western New Jersey's Quaker influences aligned her with Pennsylvania in terms of temperament and folk life.

Pennsylvania

The charter of Pennsylvania was given to William Penn, an Anglican converted to Quaker, and a large number of Quakers settled there. The pacifist Quakers controlled the tenor and laws of Pennsylvania until 1756, when they gave up their seats rather than vote to support the French and Indian War. Like the Quakers in Rhode Island, Pennsylvanian Quakers practiced religious tolerance in their lands, and small groups of Baptists and Catholics found refuge there. There was even a settlement of Jews and Turks in colonial Pennsylvania, and it was the German Quakers who invited the first Mennonite colony to settle there.

Of the groups in Pennsylvania, the Germans made the largest contribution to the colony's folk culture. The German immigration to parts of New York and Pennsylvania shaped the personality of the middle colonies in several ways. Many Germans belonged to the Lutheran churches—a faith that retained All Hallows in its annual calendar. (Lutherans broke from Catholicism at the start of the Reformation, but still used the saints' days in the Roman church calendar.) The smaller sects of German Catholics and Moravians also celebrated Roman Catholic holidays.

Perhaps the most colorful group of Germans to settle the middle colonies were known as the Pennsylvania Dutch. Their folklore accounts for the health of magic and old-world customs in their part of the New World. Their Christmas, for example, included superstitions and customs similar to those of pagan Halloween. A feast followed Christmas religious services, and prosperous people invited the poor in or delivered food to them. German children also delighted in mischief on Christmas. They "barred out the schoolmaster," a game in which children went to school early and used every trick possible to keep their teacher out until he promised them the day off and a sweet.[32] Christmas was also shrouded in the supernatural—cattle allegedly could be heard talking on Christmas Eve—and there was a good bit of drunken mumming attached to the day.

Pennsylvania Germans believed in witches and put horseshoes or broomsticks across their doors to keep them out. They also thought a witch could be killed by shooting silver bullets at his or her likeness.[33] Unlike the witch lore of New England, Germanic witch lore and superstition had the exotic character of the Catholic countries of Europe. These witches reveled at bloody sabbaths—orgiastic midnight meetings full of nudity, sacrifice and dancing. If the sabbath took place far from home, people assumed the witch covered herself with "flying oil" (most often concocted from the fat of young children, belladonna, soot and a host of other hellish or hallucinogenic substances) and rode her broomstick. This vivid rendering of witchcraft managed to last through the years, so that the image of a witch dressed in black and riding a broomstick across a full, fat moon is common even today.

Healing, psychic readings and even some black magic were the province of Pennsylvania German powwow men. These conjurers were Bible believers who felt themselves supernaturally endowed with psychic and magical powers. They operated with a book of spells—just as the irreligious witch—and could hex, make charms and cure with herbal medicines. One particular charm used by Germans is similar to the futuring rites of old European Halloween: "Write 'S. Solam S. Tattler S. Echogartner Gematar' on a mirror and bury it at a crossroads after sundown with the glass facing down. On the third day in the evening, remove the mirror but don't look in it until a dog or cat has looked into it first. It will then reveal the future."[34]

Mystical ideas, supernatural phenomena, witches and magic were a part of Pennsylvania from the very start. As early as 1694, German mystic Johannes Kelpius established a settlement near Philadelphia that recognized astrology, Hermeticism (a religion based on the occult), and even the Rosicrucian movement (one based on psychic and spiritual enlightenment).[35] Another Pennsylvanian, Daniel Leeds, was banished from the Quakers for his radical occultism. Leeds had published German mystical works and astrological predictions, and had advised his almanac readers to gather herbs only when certain planetary junctures were present. In Chester County, Pennsylvania, in 1695, court records document the Quakers' efforts to stop a Phillip Roman Jr. and his brother from using astrology, geomancy and chiromancy. The Quakers prosecuted Roman for using the occult to take "...the wife of Henry Hastings away from her husband and children." He was fined five pounds. Also in Chester County, magistrates recorded a trial involving "cunning men" or wise men who could find lost objects using occult means.[36]

Evidence of Pennsylvania's occult superstition exists even today, where barns in western Pennsylvania still display hex signs to ward off evil spirits.

Another strong presence in the middle colonies was a group of Presbyterian settlers, the Scottish-Irish. These were a community of Scottish farmers who had settled in Ulster, Ireland, and emigrated from there to

America. Their religion rejected the adoration of saints' relics and the celebration of Catholic saints' days such as Hallowmas, but their folk history with regard to Halloween was one of the most direct. The Scottish, Celtic in their roots, had celebrated Samhain, and then Halloween, for centuries.

One of the most popular old-world Scottish customs of the time was "guising" on All Hallows' Eve. Guisers—groups of young men in disguise—were found all over the Scottish countryside in the 16th century, and guising persisted there among the younger children well into the 20th century. It is easy to see the seeds of the American Halloween custom of trick or treating in the following description of Scottish guising:

> The wee shoppies in the back street do a brisk trade in squibs and "fausse faces" [masks]. As soon as it is dark, small, fantastically clad figures wearing grotesque masks emerge from their homes, carrying turnips lanterns or kail-runt torches and forming into little groups or processions, they pass through the village streets singing one of their favorite rhymes:
>
> > "Halloween! A nicht o' tine!
> > A can'le in a custock!"
>
> Emboldened by disguise, they go from door to door with a "Please to help the guisers" and are rewarded with apples, nuts and copper coins.[37]

Delaware

Although Henry Hudson claimed Delaware for the Dutch, its first tiny settlements were unsuccessful. The Swedes and Dutch jointly formed a company to establish a settlement at Wilmington known as Fort Christina. While the Swedes and Dutch fought over the land's burgeoning fur trade, Governor Stuyvesant attacked, and the colony became a dependency of New Netherland. In 1663 it came under the jurisdiction of Amsterdam, and the very next year was seized by England and the Duke of York. The duke eventually gave the lands to William Penn. It wasn't until 1767 that the boundaries of the colony were finally settled.

As a result of this cultural and economic tugging, Delaware (or New Sweden) was influenced by Dutch immigrants from New York as well as its large population of Swedes. The Swedish contingent tended to be Lutheran, and a Lutheran church was build in Delaware very early in the 17th century. Like the German Lutherans, Swedish Lutherans kept the saints' feasts in their church calendar; they celebrated Christmas as a major holiday, and remembered All Saints' Day as well.

Maryland

English Catholics brought their undiluted celebration of Hallowmas to the middle colony of Maryland. Maryland was founded by Lord Baltimore and named for the Catholic queen of Charles I, Henrietta Maria. Catholic refugees from England were welcome in Maryland (as they were in Pennsylvania and Rhode Island) and many sought respite from Protestant persecution. In 1649, Maryland's Act of Toleration officially gave freedom of conscience to the Roman Catholics, Puritans and Quakers who had settled there. Catholicism remained the prevalent religion in the colony well into the 17th century, when Puritans overthrew the government and prosecuted those of Catholic faith. In 1688, the Puritans were ousted, the colony reverted to English rule, and within four years, the Anglican Church was established in Maryland. Still, the majority of Catholics in the new colonies remained there and continued to observe Hallowmas each fall. And since Catholics and Anglicans both recognized saints' feasts, Maryland is the one middle colony with a continuous, uninterrupted history of the observance of all All Saints' Day and All Hallows' Eve.

North Carolina

The southern colonies shared with Maryland the same uninterrupted religious observance of Hallowmas. North Carolina was originally settled by the English, who remained staunchly Anglican and persecuted anyone not of the Anglican communion. The feast of All Saints was celebrated alongside the feasts of Saint Andrew, Saint Patrick, Saint David and Saint George, with drinking and speech making.[38] Religion, however, was not nearly as strong a force in the shaping the personality of the South as it had been in the North.

The southern colonies were largely rural. Sermons and churches were few and far between, and colonists were more apt to follow their old-world folkways than churchways. Also, black slaves captured in Africa were brought to the South in great numbers, and African superstition became a major force in the occult thinking of colonial whites. The African's belief in an active and interactive spirit world was firm. They believed, as the old Celts had, that the spirits of the dead rose from their graves and visited the living. African contributions to spirit lore and superstition would become essential to the unique character of American Halloween celebrations in the South.

South Carolina

Catholicism, Anglicanism and magic were formative forces in the genesis of the religious thinking of the southern seaboard. Spanish Catholics brought a Hallowmas celebration to the colony of South Carolina and the land now known as Florida. (The first Spanish mission was built in Saint Augustine, Florida, in 1565—long before the Puritans looked to the wilderness of North America for religious freedom.) By 1719, South Carolina had become a British colony and Anglicanism its official religion.

Well after Salem's hysteria had quieted and died, Chief Justice Nicholas Trott of South Carolina charged his grand jury to prosecute witches actively. Like the Puritan judges in the Northeast, he believed the strength of the occult (or any disorder within the community) was a threat to religion in his colony.[40]

The only known manuscript of occult cures to survive from early colonial America was compiled in South Carolina. The *Witchcraft Book* details English occult charms and includes remedies using human urine to cure ailments and protect cattle from harm by witches. A sick cow could be cured, for example, if the owner would "...take a heather belonging to a box of Iron, put it in the fire, and make it Red hot [and then] take the milk of cows thats hurt [sic] [and] power [i.e., pour] on the hot iron repeating the names of the blessed trinity."[39]

Georgia

Missions of Franciscans and Jesuits settled the southernmost colony, Georgia, a large tract of land that included parts of the Louisiana and Florida territories as well. The Catholic practices of these areas gradually lost importance as the colonies came under English rule. Georgia was officially established in 1732 as a refuge for Protestants from England and the Continent. Florida remained Franciscan as late as 1763, when the land passed into English hands and Catholicism was superseded.

Again, the major influences on Halloween in this colony were from African blacks and the English settlers who worked the farms in this scarcely populated wilderness. Georgia's Catholic population was nominal, and again, the matter of going to church—even if a priest or minister could be found—was not foremost in the southern frontier farmer's mind.

*   *   *

A certain acceptance of magic certainly cultivated a climate receptive to Halloween in America. From the German Pennsylvania Dutch to the African blacks, from early American mystics in Virginia, South Carolina and Pennsylvania to an isolated settlement of adolescent girls in Salem, Massachusetts, colonists practiced little sorceries and held onto beliefs that had once been the province of European folklore. The continued acknowledgment of All Saints' and All Souls' Days kept alive the spirit and law of an annual commemoration of the dead: from the Carolinas up through Virginia and Maryland, even to parts of New England, the existence of Anglican and Catholic settlements ensured the continuity of Hallowmas in the New World. The fondness for holidays shown by the Dutch, with their New Year's masquerades and Shrovetide mumming, and the English, with their Guy Fawkes mumming, masquerades, fires and pumpkins, contributed to a tradition of celebrations that paved the way for American Halloween.

As the original thirteen colonies grew, a colorful patchwork of folk superstition and autumn festivities began to synthesize into a new, quintessentially American celebration.

Notes

1. E.C.R. Lamburn, *Anglican Services*, W. Knott & Sons, London, 1963, p. 276.
2. Jon Butler, "Magic, Astrology and the Early American Religious Heritage 1600-1760," *American Historical Review*, Volume 84, April 1949, p. 317.
3. Ibid., p. 343.
4. Ibid., pp. 327-328.
5. Ibid., p. 333.
6. Charles M. Andrews, *Colonial Folkways/A Chronicle of Life in the Reign of the Georges*, Volume 9, The Chronicles of America Series, Yale University Press, New Haven, Connecticut, 1919, pp. 121-122.
7. Ibid., p. 128
8. Diana Karter Appelbaum, *Thanksgiving: An American Holiday, An American History*, Facts On File, New York, 1984, p. 29.
9. William DeLoss Love, Jr., *Fast and Thanksgiving Days of New England*, Houghton Mifflin, Boston, 1895, p. 26.
10. Ibid., p. 418.
11. Mary Caroline Crawford, *Social Life in Old New England*, Little Brown & Co., Boston, 1914, p. 490.
12. Alice Morse Earle, *Customs and Fashions in Old New England*, Charles Scribner & Sons, New York, 1893, pp. 229-30.
13. Ibid., p. 229.
14. Ibid., p. 229.
15. It is important to discriminate between the witch of folklore and the practitioner of the ancient religion of Witchcraft. Folkloric witches are the product of imagination—crusty old crones dressed in pointed black hats riding on broomsticks—and are attributed any number of mythological powers. The religion of Witchcraft embraces animism, polytheism, and the belief that nature and divinity are inseparable. Older than Catholicism, the religion of Witchcraft has recently enjoyed a renaissance in America.
16. It is interesting to note that the admissibility of "spectral evidence" (a shape outside the body of a witch) was a point of great discussion among Puritan judges and clergy. The Puritans were hesitant to acknowledge the existence of invisible fairies or goblins, but some freely admitted to seeing and wrestling with the spectral shapes of Satan's henchmen and women.

17. When thinking of the witchcraft hysteria of 1692 it is interesting to remember that the charter of Massachusetts Bay Colony had been revoked with the ascension of Charles II, and the colony had no binding laws, courts or justices until October 1692. The loss of the charter made all land titles invalid and colonists sometimes accused neighbors of witchcraft in order to seize their lands.

18. Richard M. Dorson, *America in Legend: Folklore from the Colonial Period to the Present*, Pantheon Books, New York, 1973, p. 26.

19. Butler, "Magic, Astrology and the Early American Religious Heritage 1600-1760," p. 317.

20. Ibid., pp. 341-42.

21. Marion L. Starkey, *The Devil in Massachusetts*, Doubleday/Anchor, Garden City, N.Y., 1969, pp. 34-35.

22. Samuel Adams Drake, *A Book of New England Legends and Folklore*, Roberts Brothers, Boston, 1884, p. 14.

23. Ibid., p. 14.

24. Walter Tittle, *Colonial Holidays*, Doubleday Page and Co., New York, 1910, p. 128.

25. Alice Morse Earle, *Colonial Dames and Goodwives*, Ungar Publishing Co., New York, 1962, p. 103.

26. Earle, *Customs and Fashions in Old New England*, p. 228.

27. Tittle, *Colonial Holidays*, p. 190.

28. Alice Morse Earle, *Colonial Days in Old New York*, Singing Tree Press, Detroit, Michigan, 1968, p. 189.

29. Ibid., p. 193.

30. Ibid., pp. 191-92.

31. Tittle, *Colonial Holidays*, p. 29.

32. Mildred Jordan, *The Distelfink Country of the Pennsylvania Dutch*, Crown Publishers, New York, 1978, p. 137.

33. Oscar Kuhns, *The German and Swiss Settlements of Colonial Pennsylvania: A Study of the So-Called Pennsylvania Dutch*, Henry Holt & Co., New York, 1901, p. 106.

34. Jordan, *The Distelfink Country of the Pennsylvania Dutch*, p. 150.

35. Butler, "Magic, Astrology and the Early American Religious Heritage 1600-1760," p. 325.

36. Ibid., pp. 331-34.

37. F. Marian McNeill, *Halloween/Its Origins, Rites and Ceremonies in the Scottish Tradition*, Albyn Press, Edinburgh, Scotland, 1970, pp. 30-31.

38. Andrews, *Colonial Folkways/A Chronicle of Life in the Reign of the Georges*, p. 128.
39. Butler, "Magic, Astrology and the Early American Religious Heritage 1600-1760," p. 335.
40. Ibid., p. 337.

An Autumnal
Feast in the
New Nation _____ 3

The American Revolution loosened the Puritan hold on the spirit of young America. The new Constitution protected the rights of all religious faiths, putting an end to legal prosecution of individuals based on religious convictions. Quakers, Puritans, Presbyterians, Anglicans, Jews and Catholics settled in together more peaceably as the young nation grew and prospered. In addition, immigrants from many lands infused the colonies with a steady stream of new ideas throughout the early decades of the United States. People migrated westward and pioneered settlements through the Appalachians to the central parts of the country and beyond. America was growing, and her peoples—from the educated northern coastal dwellers to the restless pioneers pushing west into Arkansas and Missouri—were forging a uniquely American character. Popular celebrations began to reflect the new democratic climate of this post-Revolutionary America: they became inclusive rather than exclusive, public rather

51

The rural elements we now associate with Halloween came first from the autumn play parties of the 1800s. (Boston Public Library Photo Collection)

than private, secular more than religious, and centered around the community rather than the church.

It was in this period of new growth and vision that American Halloween celebrations took root in the popular imagination.

Play Parties

Although post-revolutionary America was populated by people from diverse cultures—German, Scottish, Swedish, Dutch, French, Native American, black and, of course, English—the Protestant ethic dominated American society and the Puritan-spawned Thanksgiving was still the major celebration of the late fall. Although early Thanksgiving bears some similarity to Halloween—an emphasis on community and charity, for example—Halloween is first and foremost the community's public celebration of its past and its future. The American harvest get-togethers called play parties were a more likely precursor to American Halloween.

It was only natural that the early colonial harvesttime get-togethers—cornhusking parties, apple-paring parties, sugaring and sorghum-making days—would gain popularity during this time of community goodwill. These task-oriented get-togethers accustomed people to convening in the fall and eventually gave way to entertainments that were held whether there was work to be done or not. An apple-paring party was a working event; an autumn play party, however, was held just for the fun of it.

The play party was a public, nondenominational event, and whole families attended. It could be held at any time, but the first of the season was usually held in the early dark of late autumn. The apple harvest had just ended and both apples and nuts were plentiful for play-party food. Ghost stories were an integral part of this autumn celebration, and tales of the ancestral dead were told and retold by elders to a spellbound crowd. Whereas in earlier colonial days divinations were done privately and in secret, communities now gathered together to play fortune-telling games. Dancing, singing, stomping and cheering went on well into the night—if not the next morning—and some later play parties featured a school pageant of sorts.

Come, all ye young people that's wending your way,
And sow your wild oats in your youthful day,
For daylight is past, the night's coming on,
So choose your partner and be marching along,
marching along.
  —Words from a play-party song, recorded in Missouri in the 19th century.

The most boisterous feature of American play parties was probably the dancing, extraordinary in view of the fact that the church still largely forbade it, and condemned the fiddle as an instrument of the Devil. Clever party-goers made music by shouting, singing, clapping and foot-tapping. They stepped and skipped two by two, whirling their partners in the first American square dances.

Many play parties took place in a community school or hall. Some were held in private homes, or best of all, in homes that were new, before any of the furniture was moved in. No one was invited to a play party; news of the entertainment was simply passed along from house to house until everyone just knew when and where it would be.

The first play party of the year will come on that Friday evening which is nearest to Halloween. The teacher will start the machinery by assigning "pieces" for each of the pupils to speak, and as the children practice their verses the word floats over the countryside that on the appointed evening the Mountain Prospect School will give an entertainment. The country schools that I know average about 12 pupils each, and these youngsters are the "moccasin telegraph" by which the coming play party is announced. That is, announced merely by connotation. The pieces will be rehearsed to any that will listen, the one-act play which will follow the pieces will be grandly enlarged upon to anyone who cares to hear. The play will be liberally sprinkled with the well-known neighborhood jests, and these selections of humor will become familiar to everyone, far and near, long before the program is given. But the play party itself seems never to come out into open conversations...[1]

The function of the play party was similar to that of early Thanksgiving, or taffy pulls, barn raisings, quiltings, sorghum or corn-popping parties— to pass along information and to serve as a meeting ground for young people. Newly settled farms were spread out, schoolhouses small and rare and the chances for social contact few and far between. Be they in rural

*Autumn play parties featured games, such as corn husking, pictured here. The husker who finds a red ear of corn gets a kiss. (*The Husking Party, *A.B. Frost, 1882, courtesy of the Boston Public Library, Print Department)*

Massachusetts, Georgia, Virginia or pioneer Arkansas, play parties contributed to a sense of community and nurtured and prodded young
romances:

> Young and old will turn at once to rainment, and the former will
> unite in demanding new outfits for the season's opening affair. The
> latter will content themselves with airing and pressing their best
> apparel and they will go about familiar tasks humming and whis-
> tling well known play party airs. The young lady of the family will
> hunt out her freckle cream and spend hours in beautifying her hands
> while the young man will pump and carry and heat tubs of water for
> baths without one word of complaint. The children will stumble
> about, mumbling studiously at their places. For three or four hours
> it will emerge from its seclusion and pretend the world is young
> again; and that folk have gathered to do it honor. It will be alive and
> boisterous, it will revel in shouting and singing and stamping, and
> it will reach a peak of mad merriment and then suddenly come to
> an end. The next day it will be again completely disguised under
> the all inclusive name, "school entertainment."[2]

Apples and Nuts

In old England, apples and nuts were seen as powerful prognosticators.
Celtic folk used them in their Halloween divination games for centuries,
and there were some Scottish, Irish and British men and women—people
from the northern parts of England—still celebrating All Hallows with
apples and nuts throughout the heyday of Guy Fawkes. These diversions
arrived intact in the New World. The night of October 31 was known in
parts of the British Isles as "Snap Apple Night" and it came to be called
this in some areas of America as well. The name came from an old game
played by tying the player's hands behind his back and having him try to
bite an apple suspended from a string. In its more daring form, a lit candle
and an apple were placed on either side of a pole suspended from the
ceiling; when the pole spun, the player had to brave the spinning flame
and bite the apple to win. Like their English ancestors before them,
Americans used apple dunking to find out who would marry first. Whoever could snag an apple from a big bucket filled with water, hands tied
behind the back, would be wed soonest.

Nuts have been used for magic since Roman times. Some Scottish and northern English people believed nuts were such powerful sorcerers that they called their October 31st celebration "Nut Crack Night." This name, too, came with the immigrants to America. Chestnuts and walnuts, both plentiful at harvesttime, were popular in early divination games. The most well-known game goes as follows: two nuts are named, each for a potential lover, and put on a grate in the fire. She who wants to known the future watches and waits. If a nut burns true and steady, it indicates the lover will have a faithful nature; if it pops in the heat, the man is not to be trusted. (It is also possible that people tossed nuts—or stones or vegetables—into the fire to scare away spooks late at night.)[3]

In the "three luggies," another Halloween game brought over from the British Isles, three bowls are placed on the floor. The first is filled with clear water, the second dirty water and the third is left empty. A person, blindfolded, dips his or her hands into one of the bowls. If the bowl with clean water is chosen, the player will marry a virgin; if the bowl with dirty water is selected, he or she will be widowed; if the empty bowl is picked, the player will live out the rest of his or her days unloved and unmarried. An American pioneer variation of the game has the bowls filled with apples (good luck, wealth or love), nuts (luck won't change) or soot (sickness, loss of love).

Ghost Stories

> And two long glasses brimmed with muscatel
> Bubble upon the table. A ghost may come.
> —*All Souls' Night*, W. B. Yeats

Late at night, after the music and shouting and game playing were done, when the moon was fully risen and the trees outside shook and rattled with an autumn wind, people gathered together around a fire and told one another tales of the silenced dead lying in graves nearby.

Ghost stories were not new to Americans. The fear and superstition that invested colonial settlers with a lusty appetite for the invisible world were still rife. New religions that blossomed in the 18th and 19th century were often resplendent with spirits (Mormons, for example, believe that there

Halloween was the one night of the year when the dead traf-
ficked with the living, probably no surprise to the man in
the chair. The tradition of telling ghost stories on Hallow-
een derives from both the Celtic belief in the rising of the
ancestral dead on October 31 and from the Christian direc-
tive to honor the souls of the departed at Hallowmas.
(Harper's Weekly, *Vol. 38, Part 2, December 15, 1894)*

are about 100 evil spirits to each one living person). To this already fertile ground, new European immigrants brought a wealth of unholy folklore from grandparents in the old country.

The telling of ghost stories on Halloween derives from both the Druids' belief that the ancestral dead arise on this night and the Christian directive to honor the souls of the departed at Hallowmas. It is a universal human trait to bring the dead back through the telling of stories, and as Dr. James George Frazer suggests, it is just as universal to associate tales of the dead with a community gathering: "...the revitalization of the community which takes place at major seasonal festivals is something that affects its entire community and not merely the contemporary generation. The ancestral dead are therefore also involved in it."[4] The telling of ghost stories at autumn play parties became essential to the American celebration of Halloween.

American ghost stories in 18th and 19th century quite naturally took on the trappings of the region or moral climate in which they were told. Witness the Jersey Devil, a beast that managed to survive in east coast ghost stories for over 250 years. One account of the birth of the Devil dates the beast to the 1730s to an unlucky Quaker family, the Leeds; in the 1740s, a Puritan clergyman supposedly exorcised the Devil out of the "child." Another version tells of a Mr. Leeds' mistreatment of a minister, who in turn prophesied the birth of the Devil to Mrs. Leeds. A Revolutionary-era version of the same story casts a British soldier as the father of the horrible Leeds Devil.[5]

Many American ghost stories evolved from actual superstitions and rituals practiced by those in the British Isles on Halloween. The accounts of a "dumb supper" that follow were found in several states in the 19th century. The dumb supper was a divination ritual performed by girls on May Day and Halloween, these being the two ideal forecasting dates in the old pagan tradition. Unmarried women cooked a meal in complete silence, then ate and waited for the ghost of their future husband to come into the room. Women in Ireland, Scotland and England took this very seriously. So, too, did Americans. A woman in Maryland relates this story of her own dumb supper:

> ...we did everything with oil at that time, no electricity, and all the lights were low and we set there by ourselves, nobody but me and this girl, just waiting for people to come in. Just at twelve o'clock, the wind commenced to blow and it blew a gale, and the lights were flickering, and we were both scared expecting something to come

in, and Pap had an old horse that he used and she come and poked
her head in the door, and I swear, we like to tore that house down
getting out of there. We like to broke the door down.[6]

In Maryland, folk history records a Halloween "ghost table"—a table set
by the fire with eggs placed for each person who wanted to know their future
spouse. At midnight, the spirit of a cat was believed to float through the door
followed by the ghostly image of a coffin. The spirit of a person would then
drift through the door and turn the egg of the person they would marry.[7]

Another important source of early American ghost stories were American blacks. In 1763, blacks numbered 230,000, a little less than 20 percent
of the total population. Blacks from Africa and the Caribbean brought a
vast body of magical beliefs and superstitions to the new nation. Ghost
stories took on the elements of Vodoun and magic in areas where black
slaves made their homes—throughout the South, in the more populous
areas of the North, and in coastal towns where slaves settled to work in
the shipping and trade industries. A ghost story set in 1792 in the Rhode
Island seacoast town of Narragansett describes the conjuring of a black
"witch," Tuggie Bannock:

> She first mixed a little flour and water into dough and stirred in the
> hairs from the cow's tail—these were the straw for her brick; then
> she moulded the dough into the shape of a heart and stuck two pins
> in for legs and two for arms;...She then, with rather a quaking heart,
> prepared to burn the project. The sprigs of southernwood from
> Bosum's door-yard, a few rusty nails, the tail of a smoked herring,
> a scrap of red flannel, a little mass of "grave dirt" that she had taken
> from one of the many graveyards that are dotted all over Nar-
> ragansett, and last of all, that chief ingredient, the prime factor in
> all negro charms—a rabbit's foot—were thrown into a pot of water
> that was hung upon the crane over a roaring fire...When the boiling
> fairly began, she commenced swaying, rocking herself backwards
> and forward, patting the floor with a heavy foot, almost dancing
> while she muttered and sung, in a low voice, a few gibberish charms
> that had been taught by her mother, Queen Abigail.[8]

The most well-known and best-loved Halloween ghost story of this
period is probably Washington Irving's *Legend of Sleepy Hollow*. Written
in 1819 after Irving spent a number of summers in New York's Catskill
Mountains, it told the tale of a lanky schoolmaster and his lust for the

money and social position of a young and beautiful pupil. Its folklore elements include a dark, autumnal night, an apparition on horseback, a horrible prank, a beautiful woman, and a pumpkin. Although the story makes no mention of the holiday, it was the first popular rendering of American Halloween.

Pranks and Mischief

> Come forth ye lass and trousered kid,
> From prisoned mischief raise the lid,
> And lift it good and high.
> —from John Kendrick Bangs' 19th-century poem "Halloween"

Goblins, imps, fairies and trolls were though to do a lot of mischief on Halloween in the British Isles. Halloween was the night the spirits were out; farmers bolted their doors and avoided walking alone late at night. For centuries, anonymous mischief was expected on October 31.

Americans had a long tradition of Halloween-related mischief-making to live up to. The most direct antecedent was the celebration of Guy Fawkes Day. Mischief Night preceded Guy Fawkes Day in England and bears a great resemblance to the Mischief Night that preceded American Halloween in may regions: "On this night children are half under the impression that lawlessness is permissible. Householder's front doors are repeatedly assaulted with bogus calls, their gates removed, the dustbin lids hoisted up lamp posts, their window panes daubed with paint, their doorknobs coated with treacle."[9]

There was a healthy tradition of troublemaking imported with the Scottish immigrants to America as well. Scottish historian F. Marian McNeill records these precocious Halloween pranks: "Doors were blocked with carts, or attacked with a fusillade of turnips. Ploughs and carts were carried off and hidden; gates were taken off their hinges and thrown into a neighbouring ditch or pond; horses were led from the stables and left in the fields a few miles away."[10]

Young men and boys in America were especially fond of practical jokes and pranks, and the emergence of Halloween as a holiday fit for mischief must have been a cause for joy. Pranks of all sorts were popular. Boys would put a man's gate in his tree or lift his wagon to the roof of the barn. Pranksters blocked roads with logs, rail fences and bales of hay. They built a pulley device from a string and a button that made rapping noises on a window while they hid, watching the maddening effects on their victim. Bags of flour were poised over doors to plummet on the first person through the doorway; sty gates disappeared, allowing pigs and cows to escape into the street; rocking chairs hung from trees.

This Scottish prank was copied in America: "Two lads stealthily approach a window, one of them carrying a bottle. One of them strikes the window with his hand; and the second instantly smashes the bottle against the wall of the house. Those inside run to the window, convinced that it had been smashed."[11]

Chalking windows and sidewalks has long been a part of American Halloween mischief. It existed in earlier days when boys would chalk a white circle on unsuspecting victims' backs. The symbolism of the circle in this Halloween custom is very ancient: in Celtic lore the emblem implied that the rule of the sun was over (the circle was a symbol of the sun god, Baal) and its use on Halloween indicated that the rule of Samhain had begun.[12]

Of course, there was the great granddaddy of all pranks, tipping the outhouse:

Grandpa Hatch was one of the first attorneys in South Dakota. He went to some kind of Methodist College. People are always talking about how rebellious youth are these days. But apparently, one Halloween there were guys going around dumping over the dean's outhouse. Unfortunately, the dean was sitting in the outhouse at the time. The dean identified them and they were about to be expelled from school and they pleaded and carried on and finally the powers that be decided that if they would buy the dean a new outhouse and put it up and build it with their own hands, then they would be reinstated in school. So they built the outhouse and they decided to have a dedication ceremony on campus. And they made a very large deal out of it and probably half the campus was there. They had a prayer and a little speech and then they decided to sing a hymn. And the hymn that they chose was a good Methodist hymn called, "I Need Thee Every Hour," and they were expelled from school.[13]

Pandora's Box

At early American play parties people celebrated events such as the change of a season or the completion of a new home. Autumn-time play parties evolved naturally from the harvest-related get-togethers held in early colonial days, and included many of the elements associated with Halloween. They lent themselves to divination games played with apples and nuts—fruit of the late autumn harvest—and to the telling of ghostly tales long associated with hearth fires and the early dark. The pranks common on both Guy Fawkes Day and European Halloween were unleashed around the autumn-time play-party. Even the element of masquerade was present in the autumn play-party pageants held in some communities.

By the mid-19th century, an annual autumn play party was a common occurrence in many parts of America. Some used it to celebrate Halloween, others knew it as a Snap Apple Night or Nut Crack Night party. To Catholics and Episcopalians the night of October 31 was still a church holiday—the eve of All Hallows.

But the celebration of Halloween was not yet national. The holiday had no official status like Thanksgiving or the Fourth of July; it was still a folk holiday acknowledged by individual faiths, and celebrated by different ethnic groups. By the turn of the 19th century, though, Halloween would take its place among America's most treasured celebrations. There was already a piece of old England in play-party apple and nut games; a patch of Ireland in the dumb suppers and ghost tables; a bit of Scottish impishness in the mischief of American boys. So, too, is it possible to see the impact of Black slaves and their beliefs on the occult folklore of the South. These influences grew exponentially as thousands upon thousands of immigrants flooded into the country with their old-world ideas and superstitions intact. To understand modern American Halloween, it is necessary to look to Europe once more, and place the Halloween customs of the immigrants in the context of their long and colorful history abroad.

Notes

1. John Greenway, *Folklore of the Great West*, American West Publishing, Palo Alto, California, 1969, p. 417.
2. Ibid., p. 417.
3. Marguerite Ickis, *The Book of Festival Holidays*, Dodd, Mead & Co., New York, 1964, p. 123.
4. Sir James George Frazer, *The New Golden Bough*, S.G. Phillips, New York, 1959, p. 396.
5. James F. McCloy and Ray Miller Jr., *The Jersey Devil*, Middle Atlantic Press, Wallingford, Pennsylvania, 1976, p. 26.
6. George Carey, *A Faraway Time and Place: Lore of the Eastern Shore*, Robert B. Luce, Washington, D.C., 1971, p. 207.
7. Ibid., pp. 207-208.
8. Alice Morse Earle, *In Old Naragansett/Romances and Realities*, Charles Scribner & Sons, New York, 1898, pp. 70-72.
9. Iona and Peter Opie, *The Lore and Language of Schoolchildren*, Clarendon Press, Oxford, England, 1959, p. 276.
10. F. Marian McNeill, *Halloween/Its Origins, Rites and Ceremonies in the Scottish Tradition*, Albyn Press, Edinburgh, Scotland, 1970, p. 37.
11. Ibid., p. 37.
12. Claudia de Lys, *A Treasury of American Superstitions*, Philosophical Library, New York, 1948, p. 366.
13. William Hatch, informant, *A Celebration of American Family Folklore* (collected from the Family Folklore Program of the Smithsonian's Festival of American Folklife, Alexandria, Virginia), Pantheon Books, New York, 1982, p. 35. The story of Grandpa Hatch's outhouse adventure was recorded many years after it happened. Much of Halloween folklore from the 18th and 19th centuries is based on oral tradition and dating the actual events is difficult. It is possible to say, however, that outhouses were tipped over in the early days of American democracy; the custom exists to this day.

The Immigration Years: Old World Customs in Melting Pot America __4

Today we associate Halloween with witches, black cats, ghosts, pumpkins, costumes, masks and trick-or-treating. Each of these features of Halloween had been established in Europe long before American colonization. The witch and black-cat associations come from the days when Druids practiced their magic arts on Samhain. Ghosts and spirits were at the heart of the holiday from the beginning—Halloween had always been a day set aside to pay tribute to the ancestral dead. The Halloween pumpkin, trick-or-treating and masquerade owe much to the folk life of the British Isles, where people carrying lanterns made from a carved-out turnip went from house to house demanding food or money. Halloween mythology endured through early Christiandom, medieval times, the

Agricultural and Industrial revolutions in Europe and even its passage to America. By the early 1800s, Halloween rituals could be found in town-wide pioneer autumn play parties and in the private superstitions and religious services of many Americans. This fledgling Halloween was given new life by an unprecedented influx of immigrants.

Between 1820 and 1870, nearly 7.4 million people entered America from countries all over the world. Every group had an occult tradition, and each had an impact on the occult traditions of America. As for Halloween, the English, Scottish-Irish, German and Irish peoples figured most prominently. Non-European peoples who were also important were black Americans and Spanish Catholics from neighboring Mexico.

The English, Scottish-Irish and Germans had already played a major role in forging the nature of the infant colonies. By the dawn of the 19th century, many had prospered and invited friends and relatives to join them in the New World. Growing communities of Germans and Scottish-Irish influenced the Midatlantic and Appalachian states; the English remained influential in the Northeast and the South. In addition, American blacks contributed to the Halloween folklore of the South and Spanish Catholics from Mexico brought their unique "Day of the Dead" celebrations to the southwestern United States.

Of all the immigrant groups to enter America, the Irish had the greatest influence on the celebration of Halloween. They came in such great numbers that the cities and regions in which they settled took on new character, new ethnicity and, in many cases, a new holiday.

The Legacy of Ireland

Famine in Ireland in 1820, and another, more devastating famine in 1846 sent thousands of Irish Catholics looking for new homes in America. It was a vast immigration: between 1825 and 1845, 700,000 Irish Catholics emigrated to North America; in just the seven famine years between 1847 and 1854, 300,000 entered the United States.

Most of these Irish immigrants were not about to pick up the plough and seed, having come to the new world to escape their own disastrous farming experience. They first settled where the cities and churches were—Boston, New York, Baltimore and Philadelphia. Puritan Boston had once housed a small Irish population; in the 19th century this popu-lation burgeoned and forever changed the character of that city. New York received a large number because it was port to the immigrant ships. Maryland, the first Catholic colony, was a natural destination for the Irish Catholics, and the tolerant Quaker Pennsylvania had always been a friend to Catholics. As more and more families came to America, the Irish were swept up in our country's westward expansion. Large groups of Irish men and women moved west to Buffalo, Chicago, Milwaukee and St. Louis; they settled in the factory towns along Lake Erie and anywhere cotton and woolen mills could be found. They worked in mines, on railroads and as domestic servants. And wherever they went, the Irish brought their Halloween folk beliefs, and Americans everywhere eagerly embraced them.

Like the Catholics who settled here in colonial times, the Irish celebrated All Saints' and All Souls' Days. But as direct descendants of the Celtic culture, they also preserved elements of their pagan Samhain in the rituals they used to celebrate Halloween in the 19th century. For hundreds of years in Ireland, groups of girls gathered together at midnight on Halloween to perform their secret divinations with apples, fire, mirrors and yarn. Halloween revelers went visiting from house to house, led only by a carved-out turnip lit with a candle. These Halloween divination games, nighttime visits and pumpkins were quickly adopted by fun-loving Americans (who had, after all, been using divination and the fruits of the harvest to celebrate their own autumn festivals). The Irish customs reinforced the embryonic American Halloween tradition and added lush detail to its symbols.

Trick or Treat

The custom of begging for food from house to house on Halloween came from the old Catholic soul-cake custom. Once charitable in nature, "souling" took a popular turn as it evolved over the years. Irish Halloween begging always involved a masquerade and some sort of good-natured bribe, but who did the begging and what they were after varied from region to region.

In Ireland's County Cork, a mummers' procession marked All Hallows. It was composed of young men, self-proclaimed ambassadors of Muck Ólla (a boar known in Irish folk tales). The leader (Láir Bhán—or white mare) wore white robes and a horse's head; the rest of the procession fell noisily behind, blowing cows' horns to announce themselves at each new house. Prosperity was promised to those who gave food, drink or money to the revelers.

HALLOW-EVE IN IRELAND

With a Fiddler, a Fire and Feasting, the Night is Spent in Merry-making

By SEUMAS MacMANUS

Author of "Donegal Fairy Stories," etc.

Illustrations by Edmund J. Sullivan

*In the 19th century, Irish tales of the supernatural came with the hundreds of thousands of immigrants to American shores. Lively ghost stories and divinations were relished by eager audiences of all ages.These illustrations are taken from a magazine description of Irish spirit lore. (*The Delineator, *November 1909, p. 409)*

ANGRY SPIRITS

In Ireland and Brittany, a ghost of the recently deceased was easily angered:

> *The* [deceased's] *room must not be swept, or dusted for fear of throwing out the soul, food should be left for it; but any vessel of water should be kept covered, lest the soul should drown in it. The spirits may be heard carrying on their ordinary occupations, weaving, ploughing, or carpentering when they make the circuit of their old dwelling and farms. They must not be spoken to or interfered with; and any passage through the house or farm that they have been accustomed to pass through must never be closed up, otherwise if the spirits meet with an obstacle, they will certainly take their revenge.*

—folk belief from the British Isles, from Eleanor Hull, Folklore of the British Isles, *Methuen & Co., London, 1928, p. 246.*

In Waterford, October 31 was known as the "night of mischief or confusion." Young men in this rural community developed their own Halloween tradition:

> They used to assemble in gangs and headed by a few hornblowers who were always chosen for the strength of their lungs, they visited all the farmers' houses in the district to levy a sort of blackmail, good-humoredly asked and good-humoredly given. The housewife, on hearing the horn, got ready some pence or bread, and there was a wild rush for the kitchen door and scramble for the latch, while the leader intoned a sort of recitative in Irish with a strong nasal twang, hoping that his identity would not be discovered.[1]

This custom of taking a masquerade from house to house and asking for food or money was once practiced in America on Guy Fawkes Day, and for some years even on Thanksgiving. The Irish Halloween masquerade proved so popular it eventually evolved into 20th-century American trick-or-treating.

Divination

While the men were out sounding their horns and drinking strong ale on Halloween night, young Irish women gathered and summoned up the realm of the spirit. Their concerns were similar to all who seek out the future: Would they be healthy or ill? Would they have a life of wealth or poverty? Most important of all, whom would they marry?

Winter was a matchmaking season in the British Isles. Those unable to find a love by the late fall were destined to spend the cold winter alone. Very early on, the excitement and romance of knowing one's future mate were Halloween's primary attraction in Ireland. It remained the most popular aspect of Halloween in both Ireland and America until this century.

Like other components of All Hallows' Eve in the British Isles, divination began as a Celtic practice. Druids intimate with both the natural and spirit worlds sacrificed animals in the Samhain fires and read the future using omens revealed in the entrails. The invisible world was closer on Halloween, and because spirits traversed several worlds, they were attributed knowledge of what was to come. This idea was translated into Christian terms after Druid times: Halloween was the one day in the year when the Devil could be solicited for help in knowing the future.

Since the very beginning, Halloween divination has relied on the elements—fire, water, wind and earth. The most potent Halloween magic has been associates with hearth fires, candles, wells, running streams, and the apples and nuts of Roman tradition.

One of the most popular old-world Halloween divinations was apple-peeling. An apple was peeled in one, long paring, then thrown over the shoulder. The paring supposedly would land in the shape of the initial of the man the girl would marry. In a variation on this age-old divination, girls stuck apple seeds, each one named for a beau, on their cheeks. The one that stuck there the longest symbolized the suitor they would marry:

Pippin, pippin I stick thee there
That thou is true thou mayst declare.

They also put apple seeds on their eyelids, their foreheads or on the stove; the first to fall or pop was always deemed unfaithful.

Haly on a cabbage stalk, and haly on a bean,
Haly on a cabbage stalk to-morrow's Hallow e'en.
                            —Folk rhyme [Haly is short for Hail Mary]

Cabbage and kale, unlikely magical tools that they may seem, were assumed by the Irish to possess great fortune-telling power. The foods were plentiful throughout the British Isles, and young people pulled up kale plants to judge the nature of their future spouses from the taste (a bitter stalk meant a bitter mate), the shape (straight or curved, indicating the condition of the spine), and the amount of dirt clinging to the root (degree of wealth). The divination worked best if the kale was stolen; it was most telling if practiced on Halloween.

On Halloween, women made a colcannon of potatoes, mashed parsnips and chopped onion, and buried in it a ring (to symbolize marriage), a thimble (spinsterhood), a doll (children) and a coin (wealth). The fate of each participant was determined by the symbol found cooked into the portion.

Yarn was also a popular divination tool with Irish girls. If a girl wound a ball of yarn, and, looking straight ahead, walked around the outside of her home repeating

Whoever will my husband be
Come wind this ball behind of me

Most Halloween-related divina-
tion traditions predicted mar-
riage. The practice of looking
into a candlelit mirror at mid-
night on All Hallow's Eve was
an old tradition from the British
Isles; it was believed that the
image of one's future husband
would appear over a woman's
shoulder at that time.
(The Atlanta Constitution,
October 31, 1897)

APPLES AND HUSBANDS

Women once pared apples and threw the peels over their shoulders, believing the peels would land in the shape of their future husband's initials.

> *I pare this pippin round and round again,*
> *My sweetheart's name to flourish on the plain;*
> *I fling the unbroken paring over my head,*
> *My sweetheart's letter on the ground to read.*

> *—Author unknown*

she would see her future husband behind her holding the yarn, rewound. Girls also threw a ball of yarn into the barn, house or cellar, and wound it back repeating these lines:

> I wind, I wind, my true love to find
> The color of his hair, the clothes he will wear
> The day he is married to me.

According to the tradition, the image of the lover would appear and wind the yarn with her, but only if this was done at twelve midnight on Halloween. This conjuring could also be done by sowing hemp seed; the image of the husband or wife was supposed to appear behind the sower.

> At midnight, all the girls line up in front of a mirror. One by one each girl brushes her hair three times. While she is doing this, the man who is to be her husband is supposed to look over her shoulder. If this happens, the girl will be married within the year.
> —Halloween ritual in the British Isles[2]

The image of a future mate was often forecast in a reflective surface—a mirror, water, a windowpane—and this superstition traveled west with the Irish girls. The following divination made its way to the Midwest. Associated with May Day in Ireland (the other ideal forecasting date in the Celtic calendar), it is linked to Halloween in America:

> Lie down on your back by a well on Halloween and hold a mirror over your head so that you can see a reflection of the bottom of the well. If you are to marry, the picture of your future marriage partner will appear in the mirror.[3]

Variations of this divination exist throughout the East and Midwest—even as far west as Texas, where city girls believed the same superstition found in 19th-century Ireland: if they walked down the basement steps with a lit candle in their hand and looked over their shoulder in a mirror, they'd see the face of their future husband.

The Irish "dumb supper" was a well-loved Halloween tradition. Women for centuries had silently cooked and served (done, literally, backwards) a meal hoping that a spectral form would appear in the shape of their future love. This divination had many variations in the States,

*Irish girls once believed that if they left a wet blouse out to dry, their future husbands would visit during the night and turn the sleeve. Victorians relished the idea and tested their own luck in entertainments based on the same folklore. (*Harper's Bazar, *Vol. 41, November 1907)*

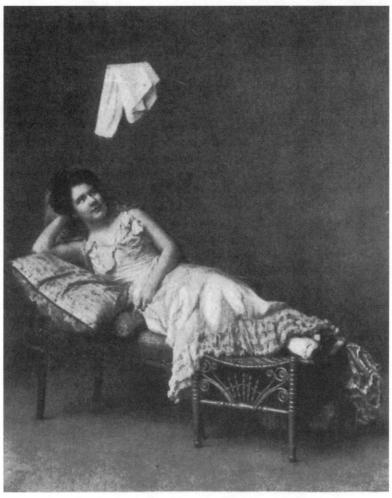

but in every form, backward motion and complete silence were essential to its success. The Irish migration to Illinois produced this variation:

> Go to a spring on Halloween, and take a mouthful of water, but do not swallow it. Then walk backwards home, get into bed backwards, and swallow the water. Your future husband will give you a drink in your dream. This entire operation must be done without speaking.[4]

Country folk in Ireland would hang a wet shirt to dry overnight, believing that the spirit of their future spouse would come and turn it. The idea that this lover would visit if a wet shirt was hung to dry appears also in the folklore of Adams County, Illinois:

> One night just before I went to bed, I trimmed my fingernails and put them in a lamp to burn, hung my shirt over the cook-stove, and the next morning when I got up there was a perfect picture of a man's face on the windowpane and it stayed there until noon. About four years after I married a man that looked just like that picture on the window-glass.[5]

Divinations done with salt and silence made sense to girls in Ireland; both had been key elements in May Day and Halloween rituals for centuries. Similar beliefs can be found among 19th-century Americans in New York state. They believed that if they swallowed a thimbleful of salt before going to bed and didn't say a word, the one they would marry would give them a drink in the night. If he came with a gold cup, he would be very rich; with a silver cup, just well-to-do; with a wooden cup, very poor.

The Great Pumpkins

Irish divination games played a large part in shaping Halloween mythology in the States, particularly in the eastern and midwestern regions. And we have seen how the masquerades and house-to-house visits of old Ireland were crucial to establishing American Halloween trick or treat. But the symbol of Halloween itself—the bright orange harvest pumpkin carved with a grin—was also a gift from Ireland.

Irish villagers once found their way through the dark of late autumn by the light of a lantern made from a turnip or beet. As time went on, groups of Halloween revelers carried these lanterns on their annual visits from house to house. In some places, they represented goblins freed from the dead.[6] In others, the lantern was not an actual turnip or beet, but any mysterious light that appeared out of nowhere and disappeared at whim. These "jack-o'-lanterns," "will-o'the-wisps" or "corpse candles" were thought to be souls of the dead, wandering interminably and leading men astray.

An *ignis fatuus* that bewitches
And leads men into pool and ditches.

—Samuel Butler, *Hudibras*

In actuality, the *ignis fatuus*, or foolish fire, is the spontaneous, combustible gas made from decaying matter; it is plentiful in marshes, cemeteries and church graveyards—or on the vast boglands of Ireland.

There are a host of stories to explain the origin of the Halloween jack-o'-lantern. The Irish claim the first, and tell the tale of Jack, a man so miserly he once tricked the Devil into turning himself into a sixpence, then snapped the money into his pocket and made the Devil promise not to come for him for a whole year. Jack lived another stingy and spiteful year, and when the Devil came back for him, Jack tricked him into climbing up a tree to pick a big, beautiful apple from a high branch. Jack quickly carved the sign of the cross in the trunk of the tree so the Devil couldn't climb down, and made him promise not to come for Jack for 10 years. When Jack died soon after, he went up to Heaven, but Saint Peter denied him entrance because of his stingy nature. Jack tried Hell, but was surprised to find that the Devil wouldn't let him in. The Devil had to keep his promise, and besides, he wasn't very fond of Jack anyway. For punishment, the nasty old man was sentenced to walk the earth forever with only a lantern made from a carved turnip and one coal from Hell to guide him.

When the Irish immigrants arrived in America, they delighted in the size and carving potential of the native pumpkin. The fat orange harvest vegetable was quickly substituted for the turnip, and the carved-out, snaggle-toothed Halloween jack-o'-lantern was born.

LEGENDARY PUMPKINS

American pumpkins were legendary in size. Irish immigrants found them more ample than turnips or beets for All Hallows' lanterns. As this Kansas tall tale testifies, pumpkins were something to be proud of.

Think of the Kansas pumpkins! Gentlemen, when I was on a farm in that glorious country I once lost three valuable cows. For three weeks I searched for them in vain and was returning home in disgust when I suddenly heard the tinkle of a cowbell. Investigation showed that the cows were inside a pumpkin, eating calmly and enjoying their commodious quarters. How did they get in you say? Well, the pumpkin vines grew rapidly there, and dragged a pumpkin over the rough ground until a hole was worn in the side, through which the cows entered. I afterwards had it cured and used it for a wagon shed.

—*from S. T. Sacket and William Koch,* Kansas Folklore, *University of Nebraska Press, Lincoln, 1961, p. 17.*

When the Irish immigrants arrived in America, they delighted in the size and carving potential of the native pumpkin. The fat orange harvest vegetable was quickly substituted for the turnip, and the carved-out, snaggle-toothed Halloween jack-o'-lantern was born.

The Scottish-Irish and German Influences in Appalachia

The Scottish-Irish formed the large group of frontiersmen who in the early 1800s, pushed from the eastern seaboard into the wilderness west of the Allegheny Mountains. There they met up with German Protestants, carving a similar path from their original settlements in Pennsylvania and New York state. These pioneers linked up a back-country civilization in and around the mountains that ran through New York, Pennsylvania, Virginia, West Virginia, the Carolinas and out toward Kentucky and Tennessee. Mountain folklore was influenced by these German and Scottish-Irish settlers, and theirs was a particularly hearty cultural stew.

Many of the old-world divinations and superstitions that originated in Celtic times existed in Scotland as well as in Ireland. Where the Irish paraded from house to house calling for ale for Muck Ólla, Scottish children masqueraded as "skeklets," or spirits, and went from house to house looking for food at Hallowmas. In the Shetland Islands, masked boys called *Groliks* visited house to house and collected money and food. At the end of the night, they gathered together in a barn and danced, sang and ate with the village girls. Scottish mischief-making had been part of Halloween for years, and divinations such as kale-pulling, yarn-winding, and apple-peeling were as popular in Scotland as in Ireland.

The Scots, however, were a rugged group of independent-minded pioneers, and holidays did not figure prominently in their way of life. They had no religious attachment to Halloween—All Saints' and All Souls' Days were not celebrations in the Presbyterian calendar. In addition, the 19th-century Scottish immigration to America was but a trickle compared to that of the Irish. The Scots settled in untamed lands, rather than cities, and lived a more rural life-style wrought with hardship and adventure. The Scots' annual celebration of Halloween was largely lost in the Appalachians. However, the folklore once associated with the holiday remained renegade.

In the mountainous backwoods, remnants of old-world Halloween divination could be found in the prevailing general superstitions. Looking into wells to see the face of a future mate, dreaming of him or her in one's sleep, and cooking food silently or backward were all rituals that could be found in the mountains. But the most vivid element of Halloween mythology in this region was witchcraft: the Scots' heritage of spirit lore in tandem with the German witch mythology produced an especially potent combination.

Witches in 19th-century Appalachia were as important to folk life as they had been to the fearful colonials. Other parts of the world may have entered the Age of Reason, but this region of America held fast to its occult beliefs and kept active a netherworld inhabited by mountain witches. The witch was to become an important symbol of modern Halloween, and her folk life in the backwoods of Appalachia is an interesting chapter in her evolution.

Mountain witchcraft was as much a fact of life as chopping wood or drawing well water. Even marriage between mortals and witches was commonplace in the folklore of this region. The following, excerpted from the story "The Devil, A Beetle and A Bleeding Toe," blends elements of old-world witchcraft with equal amounts of rural American tall tale. It tells the story of Rindy Sue Gose, a Virginia mountain witch married to Gary Ben. Rindy Sue was a "dried up, snaggle-toothed, peculiar old woman with stringy white hair and eyes like a snake."

Rindy Sue sneaked real quiet outten the bed and made a beeline torge her trunk in a corner of the room. Gary Ben opened his eyes jest wide enuf to get a good look-see, and he watched her take out a little crock from the trunk, take the kiver offen it and fetch out a little medicine bottle. She pulled out the stopper and a beetle came out in her hand. Then she grabbed that varmint nigh the witch mark on her shoulder, and hit grabbed on to hit and started suckin' blood. Whilst the beetle was a suckin' her witch mark, Rindy Sue tuk offen all her clothes and rubbed some black stuff on her from the crock. She peeled offen her skin, folded hit and put hit in the trunk. Then, she poured some awful stinkin' stuff outten annuder bottle nad rubbed hit on her hands and waved 'em in the air. Lo and behold she started drawin' up and in no time 'tall, she was 'bout the size of thet beetle. Then, her and thet beetle just sailed across the room and outten the keyhole![7]

Gary Ben gets out of bed, finds Rindy Sue's skin and rubs salt all over it. When she comes back from her revels, her skin is too shrunken up for her, and itchy and stinging to boot. She curses her pigheaded husband, kicks and screams and accidentally stubs her toe. The sight of her own blood breaks her witches' magic, and Gary Ben is able to keep her from witching from then on. Not only that, but Rindy Sue's skin, being shrunk, forces her to hobble around bent over for the rest of her days.

Because the German backwoodsmen brought the witch lore of the Continent rather than of England—that of Europe being the more vivid and sensational of the two—there was a much larger proportion of sabbath meeting tales in this region.

Take, for example, the backwoods tale of a young man who made the mistake of living with a woman and her daughter, known to be witches. He watched them prepare for their sabbath meeting and tried to follow them by duplicating their magic rituals. They smeared themselves with grease from a dish on the fireplace, chanted a rhyme, "Up the chimney and away we go," mounted black calves and rode away through the night to a sabbath full of dancing and singing.[8] The witches' magic rhymes in this story ("Over thick and thin, and away we go") are very similar to rhymes found in Europe and show the tenacity of old-world witch lore. The following variation of the rhyme was popular folk knowledge even in Shakespeare's day:

Over hill, over dale,
Through bush, through brier,
Over park, over pale,
Through flood, through fire,
I do wander everywhere.

—*A Midsummer Night's Dream*, II, i, 4–8

By 1900, accounts of witch sabbaths in the Appalachians had grown curiously American—no more the drunkenness and infant murdering of medieval European sabbaths; witches in Appalachia simply had a good old time. The following sabbath description appears in a "Jack" tale, "Jack and the Witches," and reads more like a Halloween-time play party than a sacrilegious feast:

Well, inside that house it was all lit up, and the fastest music you ever heard was goin', and the witches were laughin' and shoutin' and dancin' up and down and around and around, circlin' first one

way and then another, and swingin' and sashayin' across the middle—cuttin' all kinds of shines! Jack leaned back against the wall
and had him a time watchin' all that.[9]

Halloween in the Southern States

Ninteenth-century Southerners were especially imaginative when it came
to the occult. There were elaborate superstitions surrounding the ancestral
dead, witches, black cats and even jack-o'-lanterns. The strength of these
symbols was the result of a unique marriage between the white European
and black slave cultures.

The South was primarily settled by English in the east, and Scottish-
Irish in the western rural regions. The Halloween celebrations of the
English in the South at this time bore a great similarity to those of the Irish
and Scots. The English who had settled the southern colonies shared a
common Celtic folk heritage with their old neighbors in the British Isles.
Also, the potato famines had prompted large Irish immigrations to En-
gland as well as America, and as a result, many English emigres to
America were familiar with Irish Halloween.

The folkloric heritage of Southern blacks was African, and it included
a number of occult beliefs such as the return of the ancestral dead, the
health of an interactive spirit world, the magic of witches and the power
of charms and divinations.

Where African and European superstitions were similar, they combined
and each added credence to the other. As Newbell Niles Puckett suggests
in his comprehensive *Folk Beliefs of the Southern Negro*:

> ...those old beliefs and customs found in Africa alone either appear
> to be almost entirely replaced by European beliefs or else to remain
> almost intact in their pure African form. On the other hand, those
> found in Africa and Europe, which are sufficiently alike to indicate
> either a remote common origin or else a case of a parallelism, in
> their Afro-American form, exhibit the characteristics of both the
> above countries. Like beliefs combine into new mongrel form;
> extremely unlike beliefs refuse to mix, remaining almost entirely
> unchanged or being supplanted in their entirety.[10]

SOUTHERN FOLK RHYME

Bat! Bat! Come un' er my hat,
An I'll give you a slish of bacon,
But don't bring non yo' ole bedbugs,
If yo' don' want to git fersaken.

—from Newbell Niles Puckett,
Folk Beliefs of the Southern
Negro, *Dover Publications,*
New York, 1969, p. 353.

American blacks with a bone-steady belief in the supernatural traditions of their native Africa were ideal and willing recipients for old European folklore. Late at night in the kitchens of the South, white plantation wives of English folk heritage whispered their occult secrets to their black domestic slaves. Slave women told their children, and they in turn told their children. Inequities in the American educational system gave whites access to books and learning, which diminished their reliance on superstition, and left the American black with an oral tradition that supported such lore and legend. As a result, Southern blacks held onto European Halloween superstitions and customs long after the Southern whites had turned to other, less spiritual aspects of the holiday. They also added more of their own personal character to the Halloween beliefs they inherited than any other imported culture.

The Influence of Vodoun

Vodoun was important to the formulation of Halloween mythology in the South in several areas—witchcraft, charms and the ancestral dead. Once a religious magic system practiced by python worshipers in West Africa, Vodoun was imported to the United States via the black slave trade. Practitioners were captured and shipped to the Caribbean and the American colonies throughout America's early days. During the early 19th century, many Cubans and Haitians fled to New Orleans, strengthening the Vodoun culture in the South. Vodoun (often called "voodoo" or "hoodoo" in the States) is a term that encompasses a number of slightly different mixtures of magical and traditional religions. In 19th-century America, Vodoun developed as a mixture of French Catholicism and African worshipers of the god Damballah, the serpent. Vodoun also included Santería, a Latin American mix of Catholicism and the Yoruba religion dedicated to Chango, god of fire and stone. Conjure men and root doctors were included under the term Vodoun, although these were independent practitioners of a magic system adapted by American blacks from European magic. *Bruja*, as well—the Latin American witch—was usually associated with Vodoun but was more directly related to the folk witchcraft tradition in the American Southwest.

Like the volatile mix of pagan and Catholic influences that created much of the European Halloween lore, the combination of Vodoun and Catholicism in parts of the South produced a folklore just as full of eerie ritual, magic and the supernatural. Marie Laveau for example—the 19th-century high priestess of Vodoun—was famous for feats of magic that incorporated potent symbols from each religion. On the Eve of Saint John (Midsummer's Eve), she was said to disappear into the Louisiana bayou for nine days, then walk across the water with a communion candle on her head and one in each hand. She kept a rattlesnake as a familiar, used blood and wine in her rituals and was able to communicate with spirits.[11] Of all Vodoun men and women, she was the most sought after (even Queen Victoria is said to have asked for her help).

The spiritual center of Vodoun culture was French Catholic New Orleans, but its practice was not restricted to Catholic blacks. Vodoun was widely used throughout the American black community as a means to secure husbands, to return unfaithful husbands or wives and for revenge.

Over the course of the 19th century, some Vodoun beliefs were assimilated into the European folklore, producing an especially spicy Halloween mythology in terms of spirits, divination and witchcraft.

The Ancestral Dead

The return of the ancestral dead was a fact of life among many Africans. According to Vodoun folklore, the dead visited their old homes for a few hours after midnight. If they didn't return to the graveyard by two o'clock in the morning, they were shut out and forced to wander the earth. Appeasement of the spirit world became very important, then, since Africans believed that the dead were often present and fully capable of acts of vengeance.

Blacks believed that you should never sweep out the house before a corpse was removed because you'd then be the next to die, a superstition popular in Europe as well. It made good sense to American blacks; their African ancestors believed the spirit of the corpse was nearby until properly buried, and it was more than likely that the dust flying about during sweeping would anger the deceased. In South Carolina, people even emptied cups, pans and buckets after a funeral because the spirit of the dead person would remain on the premises if encouraged by access to food and water.[12]

The similarity of European and African superstition regarding the treatment of the dead meant that some very old Halloween traditions were still practiced in the 19th-century South. In West Africa, people made offerings of food and drink— palm wine and banana beer—on the graves of their ancestors, much as the Europeans had done at Hallowmas.[13] In America, this offering was made with whiskey. New Orleans blacks cooked unsalted food for the dead on All Saints' Day.[14] And in nearby

Vicksburg, Mississippi, a black version of the European dumb supper existed as an offering to the dead:

> Two people should cook it together, neither saying a word during the process. Get some dirt from the dead person's grave and set it in a saucer in the middle of the table. Cook something such as turnip greens, that the dead person liked to eat, set the table for three and put up three chairs. Then bless the food without speaking to one another and start in silently to eat. Watch the third plate: Unseen hands will manipulate the fork and knife, greens will be taken from the dish all the time, but the chair will remain vacant. All will be well, but should you speak while your invisible guest is with you the wind will blow, the dogs bark, the chickens cackle and thunder and lightning appears to frighten you.[15]

Witchcraft

> My mamma killed me, my daddy ate me,
> My two sisters sitting under the table
> catching my bones,
> washing them in milk, wrapping them in silk,
> And burying them between two marble stones.[16]

"Washing them in milk, wrapping them in silk" is a reference to conjure bags, or witch balls—small packets of hair, bone, blood, herbs and more used in Vodoun magic. In the southern parts of the Appalachians and the South, witches inherited the primitive magic systems of the Vodoun conjurer.

In African religions, witchcraft permeated everyday life. Fires and other disasters, disease, infidelity, weather and theft as well as other crimes were allegedly all the result of witchcraft. The use of conjure bags and witch charms was one of the most effective ways both to make and break spells cast by witches. These spells were very powerful, and prepared by using only the most nauseating substances. To inflict death or disease, for example, North Carolina witches cooked "the entrails of cocks sacrificed to demons, certain horrible worms, various unspecified herbs, dead men's nails, the hair, brains, and teeth of boys who were buried unbaptized…" in a vessel made of the skull of a decapitated thief.[17]

There were as many ways to cast spells as there were to break them, and these spells became more and more Americanized as can be seen in a folk belief from North Carolina:

> To remove a witch, go to a mountain top at dawn, shoot through a handkerchief at the rising sun, curse Jehovah three times, and own the Devil as your master. When you shoot through the handkerchief, blood will fall from it.[18]

The recreations of witches in the South share some similarity with those of their northern counterparts, but their evil sport—witch riding—was more widespread. In the French Catholic subculture of Louisiana, witch riding played such an important role in the belief system that it persists today in a form called *cauchemar*, an evil spirit that wrestles the wicked in their sleep. Even Jim in *Huckleberry Finn* had a devil of a time with witch riding:

> ...the witches bewitched him and put him in a trance, and rode him all over the State, and then set him under the trees again and hung his hat on a limb to show who done it. And next time Jim told it he said they rode him down to New Orleans; and after that, everytime he told it he spread it more and more, till by and by he said they rode him all over the world, and tired him most to death, and his back was all over saddle-boils.[19]

Black Cats

> Injun meat and pumpkin pie
> Black cat scratched out the yellow cat's eye.
> —Francis P. Wightman, *Little Leather Breeches and Other Southern Rhymes*

The black cat's connection to European witchcraft (cats were often believed to be witches' familiars) gave the animal a sinister occult reputation. Like other Halloween symbols in the South, black-cat lore was especially vivid. The magic of the "black-cat bone" was one of the most widespread beliefs (the black-cat bone superstition was found among many blacks of the 19th century, but also in German populations in Canada, leading Newbell Niles Puckett to suggest that the source of the South's black-cat lore was probably European[20]).

OWLS

The cat isn't the only animal associated with Halloween. There is also the nocturnal predator, the owl.

In the Middle Ages, owls were thought to be bad spirits that came to eat the souls of the dying. Its mournful cry and nocturnal flight gave the owl a disquieting reputation among superstitious folk: the cry of an owl was always said to signal impending death.

In America, a number of tactics evolved to stop the ominous hooting of an owl. In Texas, salt was thrown into the fire. In Alabama, the salt was placed on a shovel, which was put into the fire. Also in the South, a knife stuck in wood was said to help. Pockets were turned inside out; shoes were turned upside down under the bed; even a knot tied in the corner of a bedsheet was said to stifle the owl's deathly song.

Halloween's association with owls—outside of the hair-raising sounds an owl can make—may have come from the same natural phenomenon responsible for the holiday's association with bats: in the Middle Ages, bats flew over and around the witches' Samhain fires, eating mosquitoes attracted by the heat.

The black-cat bone had the power to bewitch, to make the bearer invisible and to turn wishes into reality, thereby making it very popular in the South. Finding a black cat was no problem, but choosing the right bone was a challenge. One method was to cook the cat in a graveyard, throw the bones in running water and watch for the bone that went upstream against the current. That would be the proper black-cat bone.[21] Or you could boil the flesh from the bones and pick them up, one at a time. When you touched the right bone, the cat would scream.[22]

Black superstition came north with the migration of freed slaves in the second half of the 19th century; the black-cat bone legend traveled at least as far as Illinois, where it existed in this version:

> If you want to rob a bank, get a black cat and put it in a pot of boiling water to cook. Then take the pot with the cat in it and stand in front of a looking glass and take each bone out of the cat, one at a time, taking each bone and pulling it through your lips, looking in a looking-glass all the time. You will not see yourself in the glass until the right bone goes through your lips; then you will appear in the glass. The bone that you have in your lips when your face appears, take that and carry it and you can rob a bank, just do anything, and get by as long as you have that bone.[23]

Jack-o'-lanterns

New layers were often added with each retelling of a Halloween "truth," depending on the personality and background of the teller, so that many times the source of the story or custom was eventually obscured. Take the origin of the jack-o'-lantern. Originally an Irish tale, there were several other renditions of the story circulating in America of the 1800s. Southern blacks used the Irish parable to explain why the eerie swamp light—jack-ma-lantern—eluded any who followed it..

> Grandpappy lost the path when he crossed the crick, but he saw a light and started to foller hit. The light led him 'round the hill, up the ridge and then into the thick woods. Then, he knowed he wuz lost, so he stopped and studied 'bout hit. He wuz mad as a hornet, kase he 'lowed he'd been a follerin' one of them jack-ma-lanterns. But Grandpappy knowed jest what to do. He turned all his pockets wrong side out. Then, he drawed a ring in his path, made a cross on the ground, bowed his head and sed, "In the name of the Father and

the Son and the Holy Speret, drive these witches away with their evil jack-ma-lanterns."[24]

Another version was an imaginative yarn loosely based on the old Irish legend, where Jack outwits the Devil in a battle for his soul.

Jack sold his soul to the devil up front, properly, at the crossroads at midnight and for a seven year grace period could do anything he wanted. At the end of seven years, Satan came for him. Jack—always the trickster—had put the sole of an old shoe above his door, and he asked the Devil to get it for him. The Devil reached up, Jack nailed his hand to the wall and left him hanging. After extracting the traditional promise, Jack let the Devil go. Jack eventually died, and was denied entrance to Heaven and Hell. The Devil threw a chunk of fire at him and told Jack he was too smart for him. Jack was forced to wander eternally. His only entertainment was leading people into swamps and mudholes at night.[25]

In North Carolina, this tale varies to accommodate the life-style of the Southern farmer. Here, Jack and the Devil were good friends and decide to sharecrop a farm and split the harvest. Come harvesttime, they couldn't agree on a proper way to divide up the wealth, so Jack suggested they divide each plant in two: "You take the top of the peanuts and I'll take the bottom...I'll take the top of the corn and you take the bottom...I'll take the bottom of the sweet 'taters and you, the top." And so on, until all the plants were divided up. When the Devil finally understood he'd been hoodwinked, he hurled a blinding light at Jack and threateningly warned him to keep it with him always. Jack never dared let that lantern go.[26]

Southern blacks protected themselves against jack-o'-lanterns by turning their coat pockets inside out—an old English folk remedy for encounters with bad spirits. This action was meant to disguise the victim or show the evil spirit that he or she had nothing for them. Blacks also stabbed a knife into the ground to prevent harm from a jack-o'-lantern, a charm once used in Scotland to break a spell. There was also a plethora of indigenous charms, like this approach: If the victim had an irresistible urge to follow the light of a jack-o'-lantern, it could be overcome only by "flinging [himself] down, shutting [his] eyes, holding [his] breath and plugging up [his] ears."[27]

Divination

> On Hallows' Eve, if an egg placed in front of the fire by a young
> woman is seen to sweat blood, it is a sign she will succeed in getting
> the man she loves.
>
> —folk belief from North Carolina[28]

Throughout America, divining one's future husband was the most important function of Halloween. It was only the style of the procedure and the
resources available for it that were particular to each region. As people
started farming the Mississippi Valley, as they moved into the western
parts of the Carolinas, out to Alabama and Missouri, they were forced to
find new symbols for their rituals.

A derivative of the old-world apple-peeling prophecy existed among
Southern blacks: if a girl placed a snail on a slate, she believed it would
trace the name or initial of her future husband. North Carolina girls put
cornmeal by the sides of their beds, hoping ghosts would write in it the
name of the man they would marry while they slept. A variation of the
old Irish colcannon existed in the South as well. The women there filled
a bowl with alcohol, lit it on fire and loaded it with fortunes in the shape
of figs, orange peels, raisins, almonds and dates wrapped in foil. Whoever
snatched the best prize out of the burning bowl would meet their husband
or wife within the year.

Country girls in North Carolina, in a practice derived from the old Irish
custom of looking in a mirror with a candle at midnight on Halloween,
looked into a spring with a lighted torch to see the face of their future
husband. Or they used this variation:

> When the moon is high, [a girl] must turn herself 3 times around to
> the left, then 3 times to the right, then, closing her eyes, she holds
> the mirror close to her face. Thrice she intones the following words:
> "Wenty-Sarum, You-wenty Sarum, Wenty Sarum." Then she takes
> 3 bites from the apple, swallows each morsel she has taken and
> opens her eyes. In the mirror, which is still close to her face, she
> will see a man's face.[29]

Out West

The rugged pioneers of the west left a tradition less full of tales of superstition than accounts of adventure. Perhaps in the difficult life on the prairie there was too little time for romantic love games and tests. For whatever reasons, frontiersmen in the Western states apparently preferred the tall tale to the ghost story, and very little existed there to suggest much use of Halloween symbols or superstition, much less celebrations.

The biggest exception was the influence of the Spanish in California, New Mexico, Arizona and west Texas. These lands inherited the folklore of Spanish Catholic Mexico—rich in Devil lore, witchcraft, magic and tales of the supernatural. Presidio, Texas, for example, once boasted Satan's actual dwelling place—"El Cueva del Diablo." The telling of legends built up around "the Cave of the Devil" eventually was saved for Halloween, and bonfires were lit in the region to prevent interference from witches who were said to engage in orgies on that night. The Mexican witches—or *brujas*—were known to be powerful, angry and often connected with the same love charms as African Vodoun practitioners or medieval European witches.

The mix of Spanish Catholic and Mexican Indian religious beliefs often produced a vivid occult mythology, similar in graphic intensity and violence to the European/African mixture found in the South. This folktale, for example, tells of a girl who meets the Devil himself at a dance at her local cantina:

> The girl sneaked out a window and went to El Gato with her boyfriend, and while they were dancing, she saw this good-looking man dressed in green come in. He smiled at her, and she went right over to him and danced with him for a long time. He was real good-looking, but he had a limp and he could still dance.
>
> When it was late, she decided to go home because her feet were tired, and he was going to take her. When they got outside, people heard a loud scream and ran out. The girl was all scratched and bloody on the sidewalk, and a rooster was flying down the street. As she died, she said *"Eres pata de gallo* (rooster claw)." This means that it was the devil, because he is always a cripple in the left foot. The people got out their rosaries and started saying them and ran home.[30]

The Mexican Day of the Dead

The Day of the Dead is a centuries-old Spanish Catholic tradition that exists to this day in Mexico and parts of the Southwest. Held on the eve of All Souls' Day, this historic and religious tradition remains one of the most ancient celebrations of Halloween. The Mexican Day of the Dead was, and still is, a joyous holiday and a glorious tribute to a people's affection for their ancestral dead:

> At midnight on November 1, laden with food and the materials for decorating the graves, the women and children climb the steep paths to the hillside cemetery. Over each grave is placed an arch garlanded with *zempasuchitl* and hung with *panes de muertos*. Candles are lit on each grave, their combined glow so bright that the flickering gleam lights up the lake and can be seen from the mainland.
>
> The women and children sit all night in the golden candlelight beside their gaily decked graves, giving warmth and companionship to the inhabitants. The men and grown boys linger on the outskirts of the cemetery leaning against the wall singing *alabanzas* and taking frequent nips from the bottles of *pulque* which are passed from hand to hand. When dawn comes up over Lake Patzcuaro, the women open their baskets, offer the food to heaven, to the souls of the dead, and then to each other. Well fed and happy, they leave the cemetery in the morning light.[31]

Halloween's Social Debut

Industrial America was brimming with new peoples, new influences and new ideas. Irish and Italian Americans met at church; the sons and daughters of British and French families were sent to the same schools; Dutch and Scottish farmers met at the same dry goods stores to buy supplies. Perhaps this melting pot was too dispersed and disparate for many. Perhaps the Industrial Revolution tore the bottom out of a social structure that had seemed comfortable for many. Whatever the reasons, there was a movement among the middle and upper classes in turn-of-the-century America to recapture the simplicity of an earlier time.

Country rituals such as "harvest homes" were reintroduced to industrial America, and the quainter, more entertaining aspects of holidays were

My house has four corners.	*Cuatro esquinas tiene mi casa.*
Four angels adorn it,	*Cuatro angeles que la adoran,*
Luke, Mark, John and Matthew.	*Lucas, Marcos, Juan, y Mateo.*
Neither witches, nor charmers,	*Ni brujas, ni hechiceras.*
Nor evil-doing man (can harm me)	*Ni hombre malhechor.*
In the Name of the Father,	*En el Nombre del Padre.*
And of the Son, and of	*Y del Hijo, y del*
the Holy Ghost.	*Espiritu Santo.*

Recite the above three times, and witches can neither harm you nor enter your house.

—*Spanish/American prayer to keep witches away from you at night, from Tristram P. Coffin and Hennig Cohen, editors,* Folklore in America, *from the* Journal of American Folklore, *Doubleday & Co., New York, 1966, p.111.*

recaptured by the wealthy. Americans looking to illuminate their British heritage "rediscovered" (and reinvented) Halloween divinations and customs. This was not the first time Halloween was overhauled to fit the needs of its new celebrants, but it was the first time that descriptions of the holiday and its customs were published and distributed nation-wide.

The end of the 19th century was the heyday of American magazine fiction. Many new periodicals were introduced, and circulated to an ever-increasing audience of women eager for fiction, fashion and social news. The widespread use of printed media produced a homogeneity in America—at least among the educated middle and upper classes. The phenomenon of Halloween could now be translated to the printed page. And what was once a melting cauldron of diverse Halloween traditions in America now emerged as a "new," more uniformly celebrated Victorian fete.

Notes

1. Eleanor Hull, *Folklore of the British Isles*, Methuen & Co., Ltd., London, 1928, p. 235. Originally from *Liber Poentitentialis* of Theodore, Archbishop of Canterbury.
2. G.F. Northall, *English Folk Rhymes*, Kegan Paul, Trench, Tribner & Co., reissued by Singing Tree Press, Detroit, 1968, p. 274.
3. Harry Middleton Hyatt, *Folk-Lore From Adams County, Illinois*, Memoirs of the Alma Egan Hyatt Foundation, New York, 1935, p. 358.
4. Ibid.
5. Ibid., p. 350.
6. Irish people believed goblins and fairies took the place of souls of the dead on Halloween and were set free to terrorize humans. Special precautions were taken on that night to prevent harm, such as stone lighthouses ("lanterns of the dead") lit to give protection against malicious ghosts on All Hallows Eve. After the establishment of the Church in Celtic lands, prayer was added as protection against the night. Men in Great Britain assembled in a field at midnight on Halloween and held high a torch of burning straw while they prayed for the souls of their departed friends. On some old farms in northern England these fields are called "purgatory fields."

7. Cornelia Berry, collector, "The Devil, a Beetle and a Bleeding Toe," in *The Silver Bullet and Other American Witch Stories*, edited by Hubert J. Davis, Johnathan David Publisher, 1975, pp. 16-19.

8. Emelyn Elizabeth Gardner, *Folklore from the Schoharie Hills New York*, Arno Press, New York, 1977, pp. 62-63.

9. Richard Chase, compiler, *American Folk Tales and Songs*, Dover Publications, New York, 1971, pp. 66-68. "Jack Tales" were a collection of stories about the character of clever Jack. They were European in origin.

10. Newbell Niles Puckett, *Folk Beliefs of the Southern Negro,* Dover Publications, New York, 1969, p. 166.

11. Zora Neale Hurston, *Mules and Men*, Negro University Press, New York, 1969, p. 241.

12. J. Hawkins, "An Old Mauma' Folk-Lore," *Journal of American Folklore*, Volume 9, 1896, p. 131.

13. Hurston, *Mules and Men*, p. 281.

14. Puckett, *Folk Beliefs of the Southern Negro*, p. 104.

15. Ibid., p. 103.

16. Leonard W. Roberts, *South from Hell-fer-Sartin' Kentucky Mountain Folk Tales*, Appalachian Heritage edition, Council of Southern Mountains, Inc., Berea, Kentucky, 1961, p. 92.

17. Wayland D. Hand, editor, *Popular Beliefs and Superstitions from North Carolina*, Volume VI of the *Frank C. Brown Collection of North Carolina Folklore*, Duke University Press, Durham, North Carolina, p. 120.

18. Ibid., p. 111.

19. Mark Twain, *The Adventures of Huckleberry Finn*, in *The Adventures of Huckleberry Finn, An Annotated Text, Backgrounds and Source Essays in Criticism*, edited by Sculley Bradley, W.W. Norton & Co., New York, 1961, Chapter 2, p. 10.

20. Puckett, *Folk Beliefs of the Southern Negro*, p. 257.

21. Ibid., p. 258.

22. Ibid., p. 258.

23. Harry Middleton Hyatt, *Folklore from Adams County Illinois*, p. 46.

24. Virginia Hale, collector, "Jack-Ma-Lanterns," *The Silver Bullet and Other American Witch Stories*, p. 48.

25. Puckett, *Folk Beliefs of the Southern Negro*, p. 136.

26. F. Roy Johnson, *Legends and Myths of North Carolina Roanoke-Chawan Area*, Johnson Publishing Co., Murfreesboro, North Carolina, 1971, p. 80.

27. Puckett, *Folk Beliefs of the Southern Negro,* p. 134.
28. Hand, *Popular Beliefs and Superstitions from North Carolina,* Volume VI, p. 609.
29. Ibid., pp. 597-98.
30. From *Ghost Stories from the American South* compiled and edited by W. K. McNeil, August House, Little Rock, Arkansas, 1985, p. 121. Copyright 1985 by W. K. McNeil. Reprinted by permission.
31. Ralph and Adelin Linton, *Halloween Through 20 Centuries,* Henry Schuman, New York, 1950, p. 21.

Halloween in
Victorian America _____ 5

All superstitions are foolish. To fasten a horseshoe to the door to procure good-luck, or to throw salt over the shoulder to prevent ill; to be glad to have first seen a new moon over the right; or sad to be sitting 13 at table; to turn twice around before setting out a second time; to frame a mental wish after speaking simultaneously the same words with another, are practices unworthy of our day, making children of grown people and fools of boys and girls. Religion is one thing; superstition another. The two are opposites. The former pays honor to God; the latter does homage to Ignorance.

—"Legends and Superstitions," *St. Nicholas Magazine*,
November 1874

Americans of the Victorian era were nothing if not rational and genteel. They were a society very recently impressed by the inventions of the typewriter and the telephone and the writings of Charles Darwin, not one to embrace the superstitions and folkways of their uneducated forebears. Yet the Victorians preserved Halloween, albeit in their own peculiar form,

*Well-heeled Victorians trans-
formed Halloween into a romantic celebration for young adults.
Here, two women daintily bob
for apples to determine who
would marry first. (*Atlanta Constitution, *October 31, 1897)*

LADS AND LASSIES,
ALL HALLOWEEN IS HERE

as the one day a year when Snap-Apple rituals of bygone years were celebrated rather than scorned.

Halloween made its debut into proper society in the 1870s. Although by now Halloween superstitions and conjuring existed among many ethnic groups, the holiday was reinterpreted as the quaint practice of the English.

Articles summarizing the genesis of Halloween found their way into the media through brief "historical" pieces published in children's and ladies' periodicals. Newspapers in the Northeast and South carried similar articles (mostly in the 1880s and 1890s). In the fiction of the time Halloween was often presented as a holiday brought to America by the northern English and preserved by the upper classes in New England. Its practice was not necessarily encouraged, but Halloween did receive enough column space to satisfy a readership eager for "new" ancient rituals, queer historical facts and romance.

One of the first mentions of Halloween appears in *Godey's Lady's Book* in October of 1872:

> HALLOWE'EN—Time in its ever-onward course, has once more brought us to the month in which this festival occurs. About the day itself there is nothing in any wise peculiar or worthy of notice, but since time almost immemorial All Hallow Eve, or Halloween, has formed the subject theme of fireside chat and published story.

The author of this article reluctantly provides his readers with a synopsis of the holiday as described in Robert Burns' "Hallowe'en" (a poem in the Scottish dialect that describes in great detail the divination rites and images of Halloween in Scotland), concluding that the celebration is simply an ethnic one "amongst the old-style English, Irish, Scotch and Welsh residents":

> Amongst the American people but little other sport is indulged in than the drinking by the country folk, of hard cider, and the masticating of indigestible "crullers," or "doughnuts." The gamlins make use of the festival to batter down panels, dislocate bell-wires, unhinge gates, destroy cabbage patches, and raise a row generally.

HALLOWEEN

Now, when the owl makes wild ado
With his sad tu-whit tu-who,
'Tis the night for erie [sic] things,
When shadows from unearthly wings
Born in umbrageous solitude
Gloom the meadow and the wood.

But still around the rustic fire,
In spite of spirits dark and dire,
Is heard a joyful, frolic noise
Of half a score of girls and boys
Over the nut and apple games
Commingled with their mated names.

Others—although the chimney roars
Its ancient welcome—out-of-doors
Run to the oat-stack or the barn;
Untwisting, some, a ball of yarn;
Or seeking in the spectral brook
Some telltale apparition's look.

No end of schemes were there of old
By which love's tender charms were told;
And still may fairies intervene
To bless the fates of Halloween.

—from Harper's Weekly, Vol. 39, No.
2033, December 7, 1895, p. 1069.

*Halloween was considered a
quaint, safe and entertaining
holiday at the turn of the century. Lovely images like this one
of children listening for voices
on the Hallomas wind seemed
less stark and eerie than earlier
conjurings of the ancestral
dead. (*St. Nicholas Magazine,
Vol. 13, Pt. 1, November 1885)

If the destructive element of Halloween was distasteful to Victorians, its Irish history was probably more so. Strong anti-Catholic editorials were published in *Harper's Weekly* as late as 1875, suggesting Catholicism wasto blame for a breakdown in America moral structure. The genteel upper classes preferred to remember that their ancestors in Northern England, rather than thousands of Irish Catholic immigrants, brought Halloween to America, and that All Saints' Day was an Episcopalian religious day instead of a Catholic one. Episcopalians hailed from the mother Church of England, infinitely preferable to the Irish Catholic church, and were perfectly acceptable in terms of ethnic heritage.

Over the next 30 years Episcopal All Saints' Day celebrations grew more public and more popular. Although the Catholic church celebrated All Saints' Day in accordance with its years of history and heritage, it simply did not receive as much acknowledgment in the press. As a result, vast numbers of American readers came to understand All Saints' Day as Episcopalian in origin. (It is no wonder, given the nature of the editors of many periodicals and papers at this time, that a large group of independent Irish and black newspapers suddenly began to appear in the cities.) In the South, Episcopalian All Saints' Day celebrations were reported to the general public, calling to mind descriptions of medieval Halloweens in the churchyards of small Welsh or Irish villages. An Atlanta newspaper noted in 1895:

> The Episcopalians in the city will observe All Saints' Day this year with special devotional services, which will be conducted at 10 in the morning...when prayers will be offered for the souls of the faithful and departed. The names of the faithful of these parishioners who have died within the past year will be read in the churches and more especially for the rest of their souls will the prayers be offered. The Episcopalians of the city usually take great interest in the observance of this day and it is expected that large congregations will attend the services.[1]

The Victorian middle classes emulated the upper classes, and the periodicals they both were offered reflected the feelings of old New England stock. On the other hand, history was remembered differently in cities such as Boston, where a majority of Irish made their homes. In the *Boston Daily Globe* of October 31, 1884, Halloween was given a rare good notice and described with accuracy by an Irish journalist in an article entitled "Why Thousands Will Think of Erin Tonight." The excerpt that follows described Halloween in Ireland, but could just as easily describe the late-autumn play parties in the small villages of rural America:

> To be sure it is a fast night, as is customary on the eve preceding great holidays of the church, but in the evening it is one which, like our own New England Fast day, knocks all religious or pious canons into smithereens as the lads and lasses enter into the fast and furious fun of its time-honored observance.
>
> This is the season there when the well-to-do country cousins send to their relatives in the towns presents of the richest products of the farm, much of them intended for the components of the savory and hearty Colcannon feast…Occasionally parties of young men and their sweethearts made the rounds of the houses of their relatives and friends on Halloween, participating in the fun and all joining at the residence of some one favored with a dwelling of more suitable size for the accommodation of those participating in the fun and Fast day feasting.

The Reinvention of Halloween

To the Victorians, Halloween needed to be subdued, to be made safe for the adults and children of America—a holiday not concerned with death or destruction, witchcraft or walking dead, but with entertainments and games that could pass muster at any society party; a holiday not of Irish Catholic origin, but of quaint Scottish or old English descent; a holiday not for the lower classes, but for the upper classes.

Children's magazines printed pretty pictures of fairies and witches; ladies' periodicals became concerned with how a Halloween party was given—decorating ideas, what foods to serve, how to break the ice. In 1881, *St. Nicholas Magazine* intoned a death knell for the old-world holiday, forever transferring Halloween from the realm of ancient superstition and primitive power to the realm of jolly frolic: "…belief in magic is passing away, and the customs of All-hallow Eve have arrived at the last stage; for they have become mere sports, repeated from year to year like holiday celebrations."

Halloween's primary motive—communion with the dead—was perhaps too gruesome for the people of the 1870s and 1880s. But the Victorians were more than willing to tap the resources of the spirit world

*The rational and genteel
Victorians held little stock in superstition and the supernatural.
They did, however, revel in for-
tunetelling games as entertainment. (*Frank Leslie's Lady's
Magazine, *Vol. 6, No. 1, July
1882)*

to know the future, particularly when it came to romance. Children were not really the focus of Halloween fun in the Victorian era. The holiday was much more useful to young people in love.

Sentiment sold magazines. *Godey's Lady's Book, Harper's Weekly, Harper's Bazar* (sic) and several others were loaded with heartbreaking love stories and advice columns alongside the dress patterns and household hints (such as how to make a purse out of a pumpkin). The early issues of *Ladies' Home Journal* were famous for their intimacy and were designed to appeal to a growing middle-class readership. Both magazines and newspapers of this period grew in size and circulation and contained more filler: more poetry, fiction and folklore—and now such material was reaching a national audience.

Victorian periodicals portrayed Halloween as a night for delicious mystery and childlike divinations, and the American public accepted the holiday as such. As a result, the holiday was primarily known for its divination games. Its charitable aspects, the companionable visits from house to house, its masquerades and provisions for the dead lay buried in the bottom drawer of a lace-filled Victorian armoire for the next few decades.

Halloween celebrations in the Victorian age seem to be made of one part romantic inspiration, one part reconstructed history, and one part Victorian marketing. Halloween ghost stories became almost operatic with regard to passion, and less concerned with actual ghosts than ever before. In and amongst the stories offered to female readers, which had such titles as "Love's Seed-time and Harvest," "Love Lies A-Bleeding" and "If I Were a Man I'd Shoot Myself," lie gems like "The Hallow-e'en Sensation at Gov'ner Dering's." In this tale the heroine is determined to live loveless because she believes the man she loves does not care for her. She takes up a dare to go into a dark, secret passage on Halloween night.

A l'inconnu! [To the unknown!] Dear friends, wish me God-speed. If I return as I go, love-lorn and alone, then do I pronounce the promises of Hallow-e'en a false mockery and dedicate myself to works of charity for the remainder of my life; should I, however, attain that which I seek, should I discover a shadow that will lead me to a solution of this mystery, then to him shall be consecrated the self-will and obstinacy and obedience and—love of Charlotte Garrett.2

The lady disappears, the guests grow fearful, but then the hero climbs into the dark after her, finding her frail form crumpled and faint from a fall. Love ensues; Halloween triumphs.

The historical divination games of Halloween were often used by
Victorian storytellers as devices to shuffle their lovers together. Heroines
ate apples at midnight on Halloween while looking in a mirror for the face
of a future husband. They followed balls of unwound yarn to dark barns
and cellars, falling helplessly into the arms of some gallant hero. They
cooked dumb suppers, attended raging, romantic bonfires, put nuts on
grates and even bobbed for apples. As evidenced by another "ladies'
magazine" tale, Halloween was but an excuse, a background, for passion
unleashed in the dark of night:

Ethel: (alone) Oh, my lost, my unknown lover! When I entered
upon the duties of a hospital reader, how little I thought that
they were to bring me in contact with the greatest happiness
and misery of my life! (turning out the lights)

(Clock strikes twelve. Ethel takes the apple and walks toward the mirror.
Door opens and a gentleman, covered with snow, enters the room.)

Mark Waring: (shaking himself) This is better luck than I expected. I though they'd all be gone to bed. There
was a light here a moment ago. (Goes toward the
fire.) It's awfully cold! I thought we'd never get
here. (Bumps into Ethel who is eating her apple
before the mirror.) Hello! I-I beg your pardon!

(Ethel turns around and screams.)

Ethel: (covering her face with her hands, starts back) It is his spirit!
Oh, I am punished for my folly. In heaven's name, leave me!

Mark: (excitedly) Do my eyes deceive me, or does this dim light
cheat me with a vision of happiness! Lady speak to me! Are
you not she who, when I lay sick and alone in a strange city
and was taken to St. Mary's Hospital, came to me like an
angel from heaven, soothing my fever with sweet dreams of
love and happiness? Are you not she whom I lost and
mourned so bitterly—speak?

Ethel: (trembling) I-I-oh, is it possible that you are here? They told
me you were dead![3]

THE CHARMS

Last night 'twas witching Hallowe'en,
Dearest; an apple russet-brown
I pared, and thrice above my crown
Whirled the long skin; they watched it keen;
I flung it far; they laughed and cried me shame—
Dearest, there lay the letter of your name!

Took I the mirror then, and crept
Down, down the creaking narrow stair;
The milk-pans caught my candle's flare,
And mice walked soft and spiders slept;
I spoke the spell, and stood the magic space,
Dearest—and in the glass I saw your face!

And then I stole out in the night
Alone; the frogs piped sweet and loud,
The moon looked through a ragged cloud;
Thrice round the house I sped me light,
Dearest; and there, methought—charm of my charms!—
You met me, kissed me, took me to your arms!

—*Emma A. Opper, from* Munsey's Magazine, *Vol. 30,*
November 1903, pp. 285–286.

*The proper Halloween party included brilliantly matched decorations. Notice the tablecloths, ornamented lampshade, jack-o'-lantern light fixtures and costumed hostess. (*Delineator, Vol. 78, *October 1911)*

ENTERTAINMENT IN OCTOBER

CONDUCTED BY RUBY ROSS GOODNOW

Mrs. Goodnow will be glad to help you with any kind of entertainment. Write her for suggestions, giving the exact date of your party, enclosing a stamped, self-addressed envelope for reply.

A HALLOWE'EN HOUSEWARMING

E HAD just moved into our new home and, of course, we wished to welcome our friends beneath our roof-tree, so we planned a Hallowe'en housewarming, which was the jolliest affair ever.

We had some little brown-prints made of the new house, and sent one of these to each of our friends enclosed in the following note:

"Our latch-string now hangs on the outside!

"Won't you come and use it on Hallowe'en, at eight o'clock?"

We invited all our friends, old and young and in-betweens. And we opened all our house—we knew that the cellar would be as interesting to Uncle John as the attic would be to Great-Aunt Martha. We had Jack-o'-lanterns on the gate-posts, and in spooky corners of the cellars, and in the attic.

All the young people were given cards, very much like dance-cards, with spaces for engagements in regular order: "9 o'clock, Mr. B——, cellar stairs; 9:30 Mr. C——, library davenport; 10, Mr. D——, kitchen-table," and so on. This arrangement of conversational "dates" kept the young people scrambling all over the house, up-stairs and down, and there was no possibility of stagnation!

And we served refreshments all over the house, too. We had a brand-new barrel of apples in the cellar; a huge pot of coffee and little squares of hot gingerbread in the kitchen; half a dozen bowls of nuts in the attic; a platter of sandwiches in the living-room; a huge bowl of fruit-punch in the dining-room; a silver dish of mints in the library and several platters of home-made candy in the various bedrooms.

At half after eleven we all met in the big living-room and ranged ourselves around the great fireplace. Then my husband very solemnly lighted the first fire on the new hearthstone, and our guests all toasted our new home. Then we told ghost stories, and roasted chestnuts, and popped corn, and counted apple-seeds until well after the charmed hour of midnight!   C. B. A.

On one hand, Halloween provided a perfect backdrop for the caprices of the upper class. On the other, the age of reason was at the doorstep, and Halloween superstition was often scorned as the practice of the ignorant. As one Victorian lady said to solace a neighbor too afraid to set a dumb supper and wait for the apparition of his future wife, "Do not try it, Mr. Oakly—if she must be not only out of her mind, but actually out of her body, to make you any response, her love is not worth having."[4]

Victorian Parties

By the 1890s newspapers like the *Hartford Daily Courant* announced Halloween under their "City Briefs" sections. Magazines printed Halloween recipes, decorating ideas and games. The norm was "quiet home parties in recognition of the quaint customs of days gone by," as reported by the *Atlanta Constitution*. Most of America had now heard of Halloween: It was an occasion for a party.

Invitations to Halloween parties had to foreshadow the fun to come. Some innovative hostesses left Jack-o'-lanterns on the doorsteps of their guests, each bearing an invitation. Others sent tiny boxes containing a handmade witch, with the invitation wrapped around her waist. As Victorian ladies were expected to be handy with crafts, most Halloween party invitations were handmade in the shape of Halloween symbols and featured a rhyming verse.

> Come at the witching hour of eight
> And let the fairies read your fate;
> Reveal to none this secret plot
> or woe—not luck—will be your lot!

The first Halloween parties were intended only for young people; it was preposterous that married couples would take an interest in the magic rites of the holiday. And like any young people's party at the turn of the century, the Halloween party was used for matchmaking. As one Halloween story attests, special care was taken to ensure that guests were able to present themselves as favorably as possible, and that there was ample opportunity for romance:

AN INVITATION

Miss Eleanor Lawrence requests the pleasure of Mr. Charles Lee's company on Wednesday, October the 31st at 8 o'clock.

She begs that he will come prepared to participate in the many stories and rites of All-hallowe'en and to wear a costume which shall be appropriate to the Occasion, representing a character of fact or fancy, one which will not be injured by communion with the spirits of the visible and invisible worlds.

—from Anna Wentworth Sears, "Games for Halloween," Harper's Bazar, *October 27, 1900, p. 1650. An invitation to a Halloween party around the turn of the century. This invitation is one of the first that formally requests a Halloween costume.*

...a splendid bonfire was soon in operation, and the gay party danced around it after the most approved fashion of boys and Indians. The sight of the flames was extremely becoming, and the young ladies had never appeared to such advantage before.[5]

At all parties, but especially at Halloween, a highly dramatic entrance was a must. The party-giver's house was completely dark, lit only by jack-o'-lanterns, fireplaces or, in some cases, long snakes made of tin and fastened above a light, whose heat made the serpent writhe. Cornhusk door knockers and silent, dark-robed figures led the guests to the cellar, the kitchen or some other darkened room before they could remove their wraps. Some hostesses greeted their guests with an old elbow glove filled with sawdust; others, with active decorations such as tall hanging ghosts or monstrous cobwebs made of yarn.

Yellow chrysanthemums were suggested for table decor in the advice columns of early 20th-century magazines, and use of these flowers was reported in the society pages of the same. Autumn leaves, cornstalks and berries adorned party rooms, and open doorways were accented with dangling apples and horseshoes.

Halloween party guests dined on nuts served in fresh cabbage shells, brilliant half-pumpkins piled with apples, purple grapes and pears, and chicken salad in hollowed-out turnip shells. Some hostesses served Scottish scones; some opted for New England's Indian pudding.

Parlor Games

Victorian parlor games drew on all of history, unearthing traditions that probably hadn't been used for centuries, such as jumping over a candle flame. The Welsh had once jumped the Samhain fires and boys in England had long ago leapt over bonfires at Midsummer's Eve. Now the Victorians, with full dress trains and tight hitched-up pants, were jumping over candle flames to determine their luck.

Parties almost always included bobbing for apples, burning nuts in the fire, mirror divinations, snap-apple, apple paring and the test of the three bowls. But there were also many modern innovations, such as a futuring game using of all things, the Bible:

SOUTHERN DIVINATIONS

A Victorian Halloween game that hails from the South is a variation on the old Celtic divination test of the mirror. In the old country, a woman would walk backwards down cellar stairs with a mirror in her hand. In the darkest part of the climb, the face of her future husband was believed to appear in the glass.

In Atlanta, Georgia in 1897, the same tradition exists, with a few Victorian effects. The woman's hair must be loosened and hang down her back for the charm to work. And she must be barefoot, for "squeaky shoes and mysteries never should go together." As she walks backwards, she must chant the following verse:

> *Auld Nature swears the lovely dears*
> *Her noble work she classes, O;*
> *Her 'prentice han' she tried on man,*
> *And then she made the lasses, 'O'.*

A man could try his luck looking into a mirror in a dark room. He would see the face of his future bride if he intoned the following rhyme:

> *To see her is to love her,*
> *And love but her forever;*
> *For nature made her what she is,*
> *And never made another.*

Numbers would then appear on his mirror, indicating the letters of the alphabet of his future love's name.

> *—from "Lads and Lassies, All Halloween Is Here,"*
> Atlanta Constitution, *October 31, 1897.*

Maidens very anxious to know something about their future husbands will do well to try the Bible trick. It's a good, old-fashioned and very popular trick. Take a Bible and place a key in it, leaving the ring protruding. While the Bible is being supported by the little fingers of two boys or girls recite these words: "If the initial of my future husband's name begins with 'A' turn, key turn." Slowly repeat the letters of the alphabet, and when the right initial is reached the key will swing around and the Bible fall.[6]

A similar party game was played by suspending a ring by a hair over a cup. The number of times it hit the side before it became still coincided with the letter of the alphabet of the future husband's name.

Young women still dropped hot lead into cold water and prophesied the career of their husbands by the shapes they saw, but gone were the days of coffins and ships. Victorian ladies instead saw books (an editor), coins (riches), pills (a doctor), and parchments (a lawyer).

Storytelling contests around the fire were given a new edge by combining the tales with an old counting-off game. Guests each took a twig and set it burning, at the same time telling an impromptu ghost story. When the fire burned through the twig, the story stopped and the next in line continued.

Another odd invention was the "test of college colors." Blindfolded girls picked one ribbon from a tangled collection of ribbons. Its color indicated the alma mater of her husband-to-be. In "Matrimonial Advice," girls wrote 100 words of advice on how to choose a wife, and the men did likewise. The advice was read aloud and prizes given to the most entertaining.

Old Halloween rites were given new twists and those new twists spawned new games, until many Halloween parlor games had absolutely nothing to do with the holiday. From the depths of Victorian imagination came a "Halloween weight test," where guests were weighed and each number in the weight was assigned a fortune. "Kissing the Blarney Stone" was a game in which blindfolded guests had to try to kiss a white stone set on a table. Young Victorians tried to bite of bags of candy hung by threads from chandeliers or doorways, and bobbed for apples using forks dropped from their full height rather than using their teeth. They carved initials on pumpkins, blindfolded each other and tried to stick a pin in an initial to determine the name of their future mate. They set tiny walnut-shell candle boats afloat in a tub of water and predicted the course of their lives based on the movements of the fragile vessels.

The myriad of new games and invented rites made something of a lean soup out of Halloween. In a never-ending attempt to throw a better party or find something new to do, Victorians added details to their celebrations that confounded the holiday's purpose. Ancient Halloween rites were forever lost among those of May Day, Midsummer's Eve and even New Year's and Christmas. On October 31, 1897, in a letter reprinted from the *Philadelphia Times*, the *Atlanta Constitution* reported the use of mistletoe as an October 31st tradition: "In this country it is a favorite evening for parties and balls, and in some sections a branch of mistletoe is suspended from the ceiling and the unfortunate girl who by accident or otherwise finds herself under the mistletoe may be kissed then and there..."

Halloween was further lost among the popular theme parties that appeared in the early 1900s. Young people gave Cinderella parties on Halloween (complete with games like picking up a burst bag of cornmeal with a sieve), Black Cat parties (here a bad-luck theme—open ladders and umbrellas to contend with in the decor), even parties with a Mother Goose theme. One of the more imaginative ideas to surface, and in fact to become a lasting part of the holiday, was the Halloween haunted house.

> The cellar had been converted into a cavern. Running water splash-
> ing over a cowbell tried under a faucet in the laundry gave the sound
> of rushing water, and kept the bell tolling dismally. Newspapers cut
> in strips and nailed to the cross beams dangled about the heads of
> the victims, and a hidden electric fan set the papers in motion and
> added breezes of damp wind to the charm of this pleasant region.
>   As each hapless one descended into the cavern, a huge paper bag
> was burst over his head, a cold, wet hand was laid on his brow...[7]

Costumes

Another Halloween custom first came back into popular practice in the late Victorian era—the use of costumes. Although Halloween disguises were still a novelty at adult parties as late as 1900, they gained popularity during the first decade of the 20th century. Halloween pageants and spectacles were also included by clever hostesses of the time:

> It was announced that couples should form for a grand march. A
> goblin bowed to a queen of hearts, a clown to a nun, and just as
> fancy seized them, gay and sober, joined hands to trip together a

Costumes first appeared at Halloween parties in the late 19th century. (Drawing by George F. Kerr, Harper's Bazar, *Vol. 38, November 1904)*

Victorians invented any number of new Halloween games to amuse themselves and their children. Here a game called "Berrying the Ghost" is played with a ghostly dummy and a chorus of mothers dressed as witches. (Good Housekeeping, *Vol. 53, October 1911)*

merry two-step in and out of the rooms, through door and portieres, a line of fantastic figures.

The music changed to a lanciers; the eight ghosts formed, the rest as they happened to be together, and all went through the figures in a way that would have amazed the originators of that dignified dance.[8]

Victorian party-goers usually took home souvenirs of the night. At Halloween they were sent home with gilded wishbones, tiny "dream pills," vegetables or even a penny for good luck.

By the end of the century the new realism was gaining momentum. Ladies' magazines took an intellectual turn: travel, politics, history and current events understandably took the places of fiction and romance to meet the needs of a changing readership. Society played an important part, but so too did the ever-increasing number of middle-class workers drawn to the industry of the cities. In the early years of the new century, grown-ups could no longer justify bobbing for apples, jumping over candles or fortune-telling.

The celebration of Halloween was given over to children.

A Children's Holiday

Some Victorian sensibility lingered through the first two decades of the 20th century, but Halloween became more and more the province of children. As such, dangerous or frightening activities were censored from parties: "Such stunts as mirror-gazing at the shivery hour of midnight, as following a thread through a dark cellar, or pulling kale stocks; none of them could be called child's play."[9] Mothers and fathers of this period lined their witches' caps with asbestos and filled their apple-bobbing tubs with lukewarm water so that no one would catch cold. If a kale stock were not available for tugging, they loaded a table with any vegetable—a turnip, beet or parsnip would do—so children would not have to go out into the chilly night air. By the 20th century, Halloween was touted as a friendly, harmless and cheerful holiday, more fun than frightening. "How-to" Halloween party books eschewed the eerie, providing instead instructional articles on children's entertainments and warning parents to avoid anything grotesque or unpleasant. In essence, Halloween's primary practitioners were growing younger and younger.

Mothers did their best to provide only benign black cats, pumpkins and ghosts; Halloween play took on the characteristics of other American games of the time. There were scavenger hunts, races, ball games, counting games, games of skill (such as hitting one of a row of cardboard pumpkins and winning a prize) or variations on musical chairs. A fortune-telling booth or wheel-of-fortune game replaced the old-world divination games the teenagers were so fond of. Halloween parties now catered to the youngest children; matchmaking games, kissing games and futuring lost their pertinence.

Notes

1. "Episcopal Church will conduct special service next Tuesday," *Atlanta Constitution*, October 31, 1895.
2. Elizabeth Phipps Train, "The Hallow-e'en Sensation at Gov'ner Dering's," *Godey's Lady's Book*, October, 1888, p. 280.
3. Griffith Wilder, "By Cupid's Trick. A Parlor Drama for All Hallowe'en," *Godey's Lady's Book*, November, 1885, pp. 500-501.
4. Ella Rodman Church, "Through a Looking-Glass," *Godey's Lady's Book*, October, 1880, p. 346.
5. Ibid., p. 345.
6. "To-Night Is Hallowe'en," *Hartford Daily Courant*, October 31, 1895, p. 6.
7. Mary McKim Marriot, "Social Affairs for Halloween," *Ladies Home Journal*, October 1908, p. 58.
8. Anna Wentworth Sears, "Games for Halloween," *Harper's Bazar*, October 27, 1900, p. 1651.
9. Isabel Gordon Curtis, "A Children's Celebration of Halloween," *St. Nicholas Magazine*, Volume 32, Part II, October, 1905, p. 1124.

Halloween in the
20th Century _____ 6

Halloween's heritage was obscured by the Victorians. By the early 20th century, people rarely associated the religious celebrations of All Saints' and All Souls' Days with their secular celebrations of Halloween. But neither was Halloween confined to upper-class parties, children's parties or to the superstitious rituals of the Old World. This was a time of new popularism, and America's growing civic organizations—Scouts', Kiwanis, Rotarians' and Lions' clubs—allied with churches and schools to promote the celebration of Halloween as an event for everyone.

A Public Celebration

Anoka, Minnesota, boasts one of the first community-wide Halloween celebrations. An annual event since 1921, the town decorates its streets, hosts two parades (one for younger children and one for the general public), holds a Pumpkin Bowl football game and ropes off a city square

*The public Halloween party, ca. 1925, in Anoka, Minnesota.
(From the collection of the Minnesota Historical Society)*

Adults and children don Halloween costumes at Anoka, Minnesota's public celebration, circa 1937. (Minnesota Historical Society)

for dancing. City officials in Allentown, Pennsylvania, arranged and sponsored their first annual Halloween parade in the early 1900s as well. The parade followed a format similar to the town's Thanksgiving and Fourth of July parades: there were bands in uniform, sports presentations and a curious mix of marchers dressed as Uncle Sams, Charlie Chaplins and ghosts. In rural Glens Falls, New York, manufacturing and retail concerns, schools and civic groups joined forces for that town's first annual Halloween parade in 1927. In midtown Manhattan, annual public Halloween parties were held on the Central Park Mall beginning in 1936. Newark, New Jersey, drew the largest crowd ever at its 1939 Halloween parade—some 300,000 people. And Halloween was such a large event in Hagerstown, Maryland, that the mayor postponed the holiday in 1936 by official proclamation. Halloween fell on a Saturday that year, and the mayor chose to move the town's annual Halloween mummers' parade to November rather than have it compete with Saturday shopping. From Evansville, Indiana, to Los Angeles, California, to Miami Beach, Florida, communities large and small marked Halloween with a civic celebration. Halloween's regional differences disappeared as America was united by newspapers, national magazines and, later, radio. Halloween was no longer a night for quiet divination and romance—it took to the streets of cities and towns—and with its prankster hordes came a host of new holiday problems.

The Halloween "Problem"

There had always been some hell-raising in Halloween, but a new brand of mischief emerged in the 20th century. Rather than overturn an outhouse or hide a sty fence, revelers were now tempted to steal, set small fires and damage property. By the 1920s, October 31st mischief became known as "the Halloween problem," and many adults began to question the need for a holiday that encouraged pranks and anarchy. What began as a good-natured tussle between children and adults on Halloween grew into a somewhat serious battle.

School officials, aided by civic and church leaders, held that the spirit of Halloween needed to be tamed. They tried to recast the holiday in an orderly, more charitable light. The *Delineator* encouraged its Boy Knights (a club of boys sponsored by the magazine) to gather food, provisions and clothes to bring to poor people on Halloween. Those with a public

As Halloween mischief became more destructive, young boys were often employed by police to help curb Halloween vandalism. (St. Nicholas Magazine, Vol. 35, October 1908)

forum—editors and journalists—echoed the need for charity on this night of devils:

> Goblins and witches are supposed to run rampant on the evening of the last day of October. Why they should is not so certain, for Hallowe'en had its inception in deeds of kindness and charity, performed by good fairies, elves, and sprites whose concern was the making of folk happy rather than miserable. Poor families were wont to find baskets of food on their doorsteps instead of rubbish; woodpiles were magically sawed and split into stove lengths.[1]

Parents were also involved in the effort to diffuse the holiday's prankish spirit. Neighborhoods came together to make refreshments—seedcakes, tarts and cider—hoping that the lure of free treats might keep children from mischief on Halloween night.

In 1925, the Chicago Principals' Club mounted a widely publicized, organized campaign to alter the nature of Halloween. Their basic idea was one that would gain credence in hundreds of American communities over the next three decades: "substitution of reputable fun for mischief." Teachers in all Chicago schools, public and parochial, gave lessons prior to Halloween geared to make children feel responsible for the safekeeping of their own city. The principals' instructions to teachers were very specific: demonstrate to the children that the money for their education comes directly from taxes paid by the same shopkeepers and home owners who are most often the victims of Halloween pranks.

Chicago police were instructed to report any children committing pranks to the Principals' Club; children themselves were asked to keep their eyes open and report any Halloween tricksters. Thousands of students were sent to clean up yards, fix fences, paint houses or dress dolls for children in the hospital. As a reward, they were invited to parties sponsored by Kiwanis, Lions' and Rotarians' clubs, churches and parent–teacher Associations. October 31 passed quietly that year. Police reported a decrease in vandalism and the city saved several thousand dollars in fire damage, thefts and damage to property.

In Oberlin, Kansas, since 1927, Halloween was set aside to rake front yards and take away leaves. The Hi-Y club went so far as to suggest that the town dispense with police on Halloween night and spend the money saved on treats for the children who had done the work. It was another successful ploy—there was very little mischief reported.

THESE PRANKS ARE NEVER MEAN . . .

Teachers instructed younger children about Halloween safety and the types of Halloween fun that were acceptable. Elementary school curricula now included pageants useful in reshaping children's thinking about Halloween:

Fourth child: ... people of long ago tell us that on one night in the year above all others the brownies hold high carnival. Then they play all sorts of funny pranks upon brownies, and upon really people too. But these pranks are never mean, they are just funny.

—elementary school recitation, 1913, from Nan L. Mildren, "A Halloween Entertainment for Rural Schools," Ladies Home Journal, *October 1913, p. 103*

A Halloween party at a private dancing school in 1935.
(Minnesota Historical Society)

In New Rochelle, New York, police enlisted local boys—the town's potential troublemakers—to patrol the streets on Halloween night. The boys were officially under contract, "guarding against tick-tacks on lower windows, painting store steps in assorted colors, carrying off cast iron dogs from gardens and ringing doorbells and running away afterwards."

Having pranksters police themselves was effective, but it wasn't the only tactic employed. In Detroit in 1935, 45,000 children were invited to 90 public Halloween parties throughout the city. The largess for this effort came from the city's administrators, who developed the idea to avoid increased traffic deaths and false fire alarms and to prevent its annual "Halloween hangover." And in 1938, the commissioner of police in Boston footed the bill for ice cream and cake at parties in 15 district police stations to distract mischief-makers from plying their art in the dark of October 31.

But despite the good attempts of many communities, the problem of vandalism persisted, especially in urban areas. In Queens, New York, for example, 1,000 windows were broken on Halloween 1939. Tires were slashed, car windshields pelted with eggs, gas caps stolen and false fire alarms rung. Such activities escalated throughout the late 1930s and nearly ruined Halloween in some cities. A plea came from the editor of the *Houston Chronicle* to civilize Halloween: "It is an unregenerate sort of day needing redemption—it can be reinterpreted in terms of a national carnival, an event which we really need in this country..."[3] Even Chicago, with its successful Halloween safety campaign of 1925, considered eliminating the holiday by 1942. America had just entered World War II, and adults everywhere were caught up in a worldwide drama that demanded vigilance and conservatism. Anything destructive or wasteful—like Halloween mischief—was treated with new seriousness. Towns called in their air wardens to help guard against vandals, and stern warnings were issued from municipal, church and especially school authorities:

Letting the air out of tires isn't fun anymore. It's sabotage. Soaping windows isn't fun this year. Your government needs soaps and greases for the war. Carting away property isn't fun this year. You may be taking something intended for scrap, or something that can't be replaced because of war shortages. Even ringing doorbells has lost its appeal because it may mean disturbing the sleep of a tired war worker who needs his rest.

—James M. Spinning, superintendent of schools, Rochester,
New York, 1942[4]

A WARTIME MEASURE

The Chicago City Council voted unanimously today to abolish Halloween for the duration and called upon Mayor Edward L. Kelly to issue a proclamation making October 31 "Conservation Day."

—New York Times, *October 15, 1942, p. 20.*

The nation's children got a good, strong message in 1942. Halloween mischief would not be tolerated as long as there was a war going on. Like many other large-scale public holidays, Halloween celebrations were altered to fit the temper of the time.

Wartime Halloween

Despite the cancellation of the holiday in some areas, there was an effort by many communities to keep up public celebrations of Halloween during World War II. It was morale-building, it was a good excuse to get together, and it gave people something else to think about for a while. It is true that Halloween vandalism infuriated some town fathers to the point that they were willing to abandon the holiday, but most communities carried on believing there was an even greater need for recreation during wartime. In New Britain, Connecticut, for example, the superintendent of schools urged the public to have private parties to make up for the cancellation of the town's customary parade: "The undersigned, therefore, strongly urge you to hold a party in your home on Halloween night for your children and their friends...You will be surprised at the fun you will get out of it. You certainly will be happy in the thought that in this small way you and your children have made a distinct contribution to our war effort."[5]

Adjustments were made. Magazines and newspapers suggested alternatives to Halloween decorating and costumes that would not deplete war resources. Because so many men were missing, new games were invented that did not rely so much on partners. Some Halloween games took on a military bent, like the test of the bowls. In the wartime version of this Halloween game, blindfolded girls chose one of seven bowls filled with different substances; red cloth, for instance, indicated they would marry an army man and a blue cloth, a sailor. In communities that had to cancel their Halloween festivities due to war shortages, new ones were invented. Centralia, Illinois, for example, did not have enough resources or marching men for their usual Halloween parade, so they made a parade out of all the organizations that were helping the war effort—the Red Cross, Boy Scouts, Air Raid Wardens, Auxiliary Fire and Policemen, the American Legion and the Veterans of Foreign Wars.

Although cities and towns tried their best during the war years, Halloween celebrations were subdued due to the great demand for resources overseas. Halloween mischief-making was seriously curtailed by a public

A MANIFESTO
War Recreation Congress
Cincinnati, Ohio
September 28–October 2, 1942

All America is now geared to one purpose—win the war. This means work—hard, long hours. It means sacrifice of accustomed comforts. It means a drain on our mental, physical and spiritual powers.

Now, of all times, the restful, rebuilding, healing, creative power of recreation must be released to all the people. Recreation is a source of spiritual power from which one returns with renewed spirit.

The recreation forces of America have heard the call. They are mobilized for total war service. Their task is to serve all people. They minister to soldier and sailor, to workers in war industries, to civilian volunteers, to children growing up under war conditions.

To meet this task and the many other wartime demands being made upon recreation leaders, we must face together the problems that have arisen since Pearl Harbor and the more pressing ones that loom ahead. It is of vital importance that every ounce of energy and time, every area and facility, all financial resources, be used wisely.

The recreation resources of America—areas, facilities, leadership— volunteers and professional—a financial investment now over six billion, all must be fully converted to the war effort.

This is the purpose of the War Recreation Congress in Cincinnati. This is why it is important for public officials, recreation leaders and laymen to set aside a few days to consider together how best this can be done. No one city has all the answers. We are a national cooperative movement. We are faced with a need requiring unified action. The Cincinnati Congress will provide the opportunity.

What are your war recreation problems? How have you converted your program? Have you found ways of replacing leaders called to the armed services? What are you doing for those serving in war industries? Are children of working parents being served? Are your facilities fully at the disposal of the armed forces?

Study your situation. Bring your answers and your questions to the War Recreation Congress in Cincinnati. Let's face them together to the end that all recreation work during the coming year may count toward winning the war.

—from Recreation Magazine, Vol. 36, October 1942—the mandate and call to action of the War Recreation Congress. Americans took organized recreation very seriously, and did what they could to keep Halloween events going during the war.

single-minded in their support of the conservation effort. But with victory, a new spirit of celebration infused the States and holidays flourished once more.

A Holiday for Everyone

Civic leaders picked up their crusade for a safe Halloween right where they had left off in 1942. The Marinette, Wisconsin, director of recreation developed his town's party to rid the city of the "nuisance" of tricksters. Marinette entertained its children (about 1,000 in 1947) from 6 to 9 p.m. (prime prank time) by renting the town's largest theater and showing movies for free. The cost to the town was $356.68, much less than the potential cost of vandalism damage. In Fort Wayne, Indiana, it was the mayor who initiated a citywide extravaganza. He organized a Mayor's Club (complete with membership cards) to which children could belong if they helped curb vandalism on Halloween. One thousand cards were issued to children enlisted to report incidents of bad citizenship. As a reward, five community "centers" were set up for the kids. Each center had a room of horrors in a pitch-black gymnasium where electrically charged slides, bedsprings, wet mops, barrels and old tires were used to create the effects of a haunted house.

Imaginative recreation departments came up with radio giveaway contests on Halloween to make sure children went directly home after their parties. Children entered their names the week before Halloween; the stations called their homes within 30 minutes after the town's festivities, and if they were home, they won. In Passaic, New Jersey, it was the commissioner of police who suggested a gigantic costume parade. The parade had become an annual event, with 5,000 costumed marchers taking part. In Newton, Massachusetts, massive Halloween celebrations throughout the 1950s served 10,000 children at 240 parties given throughout the city's schools, churches, clubs, YMCA's and private homes. The celebration operated with 1,400 volunteers, over 200 committees, and a budget written into the town's recreation-department allotment as a line item each year. The whole machine was set in motion with a letter to each parent, stating the purpose of the citywide event:

> To form a correct concept in children's minds regarding Halloween; to afford children intelligent, thoroughly pleasant, but safe, enjoy-

IS IT REAL?

"Haunted" rooms and other grotesque displays of Halloween artistry grew popular at home parties of the 30s and 40s. Halloween was expected to deliver a thrill for children, and adults were forced to grow more clever each year to succeed. Many children's parties featured games where dummied up body parts were passed or touched in the dark. A moist sponge—in the dark and with the right introduction—would make a believable human lung or brain. Dried peaches passed for ears; wet, cold boiled macaroni for a windpipe, or a scaly chicken claw slathered with thick laundry suds as a bony dead hand. The Halloween stunts performed at parties required more sophistication and skill than Halloween tricks of the past:

"Beheading of the Ghosts" proved an exciting stunt. The victims were led, one by one, into the death chamber where a boy dressed as the devil carried a huge cardboard axe over his shoulder. Each one was led by a ghost to a wooden block and made to kneel before it with his neck across it. The axeman then raised his axe and as it descended, apparently on the victim's neck, the lights were extinguished and a resounding whack was heard, followed by a scream.

—from E. V. Harbin, editor, The Fun Encyclopedia, *Abbingdon-Cokesbury Press, New York and Nashville, 1940 (Whitman & Smith), p. 735.*

ment; to spend only a limited amount of money, but enough to avoid
damage usually amounting to more than the expenditure; to direct
children's minds from mischief to healthy pastimes; to teach them
respect for other people's property; and above all, to instill in young
minds the fundamentals of good citizenship.[6]

It was not just the cooperative structure of postwar Halloween celebrations that were so all-inclusive—leagues, chambers, parents, and schools
all collaborated—it was also the numbers. These events were extremely
well attended. There were under 6,000 people in the city of Coronado,
California, in the 1940s; 700 to 1,000 of them gathered every year on the
athletic field for Halloween. In Elkhart, Indiana, in 1946, 7,000 children
attended 134 parties. In Newton, Massachusetts, one in every seven
people attended the town's Halloween parties of the 1940s and '50s.
Halloween had achieved full stature as a national holiday—its popularity
now rivaled the annual patriotic celebrations of the Fourth of July and
Memorial Day.

Toward a Truly Modern Halloween

During the postwar years, Halloween celebrations became more of a
genuine party for kids and less of a diversion for pranksters. Halloween
was now an important children's holiday in a nation that was becoming
increasingly obsessed with children. Its very popularity dictated that the
holiday alter its shape once more.

By the 1950s, America was bursting with more young children than
ever before. Large public celebrations of Halloween grew too expensive
for some communities and simply too large for others. In a way, the
campaign to make Halloween safe for the whole family had worked,[7] and
there wasn't so great a need for large, organized civic events. In the spirit
of family values that typified the '50s, the impetus for Halloween celebrations moved once more from the community to the family and school.
Classroom parties took the place of town festivities in many communities.
Mothers held Halloween parties at home for their children, much as they
had in the early 20th century. But the most important development in
Halloween at this time was the revival of an ancient Halloween ritual—
trick or treat.

Hollywood helped create the stereotype of the American witch—a hunched figure with arthritic hands, a beakish nose, wrinkles, warts and a hideous grin. (Cortlandt Hull Collection: (below) The Wizard of Oz, *© 1939 MGM-Turner Entertainment; (opposite)* Snow White and the Seven Dwarfs, *© 1937, Walt Disney Company)*

A KANSAS TOWN CELEBRATES HALLOWEEN

The idea for a civic celebration was born in 1928. In the first few years, blooded cattle were given away through registrations in the business houses; a huge choir contest was held in the park; and free games, shows, and dances were held. Since then, the celebration has grown and changed.

On the evening that Arkalalah [an Indian word meaning 'good time'] begins, there is a gala air about the town, with flags waving welcome from the lightposts, and jack-o'-lanterns decorating the store fronts. On that evening, the coronation of Queen Alalah, who reigns over the two-day gaiety, is held. She has been chosen from the girls in the sophomore class of Arkansas City Junior College...

The coronation program starts, perhaps with a fantasy of light and movement created by senior-high-school dancers. Then the grade-schoolers entertain with a lively dance of toy soldiers or balloons. A magician may be part of the program, or a clown. Whatever it is, you can depend upon singing and laughter throughout the evening. Following the pageant comes a grand march and the coronation ball.

Street contests start early the next morning downtown. Tired winners of the centipede race may be making room for the potato-sack race at one corner, while at another intersection, you'll see a circle of onlookers and hear them cheering for the terrapin derby. Perhaps there's and egg-tossing contest, a rooster race, a baby-crawling contest.

—from "Festival Time at Halloween," Recreation Magazine, *September 1956, p. 334.*

Notes

1. "Chasing the Halloween Goblins," *Educational Review*, October 1927, p. 65.
2. "50 New Rochelle Boys Act as Halloween Police," *New York Times*, November 1, 1923, p. 23.
3. "Reforming Halloween," *New York Times*, October 27, 1935, Section IV, p. 8.
4. "Hits Halloween Revels," *New York Times*, October 23, 1942, p. 16.
5. "New Britain Changes Its Plans," *Recreation Magazine*, Volume 37, October 1943, p. 384.
6. "How One City Handles Halloween," *Recreation Magazine*, Volume 44, September 1950, p. 189.
7. In 1941 the National Recreation Association published "The Community Celebrates Halloween," a study describing Halloween festivities in 20 cities of different sizes. In each case the abundance of large scale parties made for a safer Halloween (*American City*, Volume 56 October 1941, p. 99). The *Saturday Evening Post* in 1952 reported on a survey of 30 communities, and in every case Halloween vandalism was curbed almost entirely by supplying fun and refreshments (*Saturday Evening Post*, Volume 225, October 25, 1952, p. 2). Although Halloween vandalism has seen peaks and ebbs over time, it has never been completely absent. Americans still do battle on Halloween night with flaming dumpsters, thrown eggs, spray-painted cars, toppled headstones and slashed tires.

Contemporary Halloween: Old Traditions Made New   7

The jack-o'-lantern—a candle-lit beacon that recalls the roaring fires of a darker time—still lights the way for masqueraders on Halloween. The masquerade itself is part of a tradition born in ancient times and transformed for a modern public. Where once villagers masked themselves and paraded to the town's limits to drive out evil spirits, folks now don brightly colored disguises for trick or treat and giddy parades down city streets. Where once people provided food for the indigent on All Hallows, American trick or treaters now collect money for UNICEF.

Trick or Treat

It is Halloween. A group of hilarious youngsters in costume, including two Charlie Chaplins, a Topsy, a Gingerbread Man and an
Indian, noisily approach the front door of a large house, ring the bell
and when the owner herself comes to the door, greets her in chorus
with:
  Nuts! Nuts! We want nuts!
  Nuts! Nuts! We want nuts!
                —*Ladies Home Journal*, October 1920, p. 135

This is one of the earliest descriptions of Halloween trick or treating in
the national popular literature of the 20th century. Trick or treating, now
nearly synonymous with the holiday, was one of the last elements to
emerge in the celebration of American Halloween.

Trick or treating grew popular between 1920 and 1950, probably
finding its first practices in the wealthier areas of the East and slowly
spreading to remote areas of the West and South. Reports of trick-or-treaters exist in Wellesley, Massachusetts, as early as the late 1920s, but not
until the '40s in North Carolina, Florida and Texas. By the 1950s, every
child in America had heard about the custom. It became a child's right
and privilege to go house to house on Halloween, cheerfully hollering
"trick or treat!" and filling pillowcases with apples, candy and money.
They didn't need to know the history of the holiday to savor the mystery
of a cool, dark October night or the sheer thrill of begging for candy while
disguised as one's favorite fantasy or television character.

The origins of Halloween trick or treating are very old indeed. An early
American antecedent was Guy Fawkes Day. The celebration, popular in
parts of the East during the 17th and 18th centuries, died out in most
communities around the American Revolution. Thanksgiving, however,
was being celebrated with some regularity at that time, and it became a
Thanksgiving custom for children to dress up and beg from house to house
on the last Thursday in November.[1] At first the poorer children would
dress in cast-off ragged clothes and beg "something for Thanksgiving"
from their wealthier neighbors. Soon all kinds of children got involved,
and the custom grew more popular and costumes more elaborate. The
Thanksgiving masquerade existed as late as the 1930s, then suddenly
vanished, and Halloween costumes and parades began to gain national
popularity. Where once Guy Fawkes celebrants had mocked the pope, and

Thanksgiving revelers had burlesqued the rich, Halloween masqueraders would now take on politicians, movie stars, folk heroes and even religious leaders.

As for begging, the notion of receiving gifts of candy on Halloween owed something to the public parties of the previous decades. Youngsters were used to being offered goodies as incentive to stay in, to gather at a church or school, or to go right home after a party rather than ring doorbells, paint church steps or chalk windows. Trick-or-treating children now offered their potential victims a choice: if neighbors went along and gave freely of their chocolate bars and homemade cookies, they were safe. If not, there were a number of well-practiced and annoying punishments in store. Over time, the trick part of trick or treat was relegated to the night before Halloween—called Mischief Night in many communities—and the treat part to Halloween proper.

A New Twist in the Halloween Trick

In 1970, five-year-old Kevin Tostan died after allegedly eating Halloween candy laced with heroin. Investigators discovered that the heroin belonged to an uncle, and was not in a Halloween treat but in the uncle's home within reach of the boy.

On Halloween 1974, eight-year-old Timothy O'Bryan died of cyanide poisoning after eating a Halloween treat. Ronald Clark O'Bryan reported his son had become very ill after eating Pixy Stix he'd gotten from a house in nearby Pasadena, Texas. Police found that the Pasadena house had been empty on Halloween, and the truth was that Ronald O'Bryan had put enough cyanide in the Pixy Stix to kill two or three people. Unbeknownst to his wife, O'Bryan had taken out a $20,000 life insurance policy on each of his children (his daughter also had poisoned candy in her treats; police recovered it). He was convicted and sentenced to death by injection. The execution was to have taken place on Halloween 1982, but O'Bryan received a stay of execution nearly four weeks before.

These two cases are the only deaths actually attributed to Halloween-related violence in the last two decades. Rumors of candy laced with drugs also appeared as early as the 1960s. Whether these rumors were true or not, adults were willing to believe they were, and Halloween safety became an issue of national importance. By the late 1960s, the media was full of Halloween safety tips, and by the early 1970s, the public was urged

Halloween masquerades of the 20th century hearken back to the ancient Celtic custom of impersonating the restless dead. Witch Dungeon (a Connecticut museum open only on Halloween) proprietor Cortlandt Hull poses with five of his most famous creations. (Cortlandt Hull Collection)

to replace candy treats with nonedible ones (an effort supported with flyers from the Toy Manufacturers of America). The press was reporting more and more Halloween incidents, such as older children attacking younger children to steal their treats, or children finding razor blades or pieces of glass in their candy. The whole Halloween picture was polluted with fear.

Some towns questioned the need for trick or treating. Mayor John W. Fitzgerald of Burbank, Illinois, outlawed trick or treat in September 1972: "Knocking on someone's door and asking for a Halloween treat will be considered as an illegal form of solicitation."[2] The mayor cited harassment of smaller children by teenagers, and treats laced with drugs and razor blades as reasons for eliminating trick or treat. Hardwick, Massachusetts, banned trick or treat in the late 1970s, after some children reported receiving candies with razor blades hidden in them.

Then, in late September 1982, cyanide was found in Extra-Strength Tylenol capsules in the Chicago area. Seven people died and a whole nation watched as the story unfolded over the first few weeks in October. The killer was not caught, and Halloween was a fortnight away.

There was a renewed effort to ban trick or treating.[3] The Boards of Selectmen of Palmer and Holland, Massachusetts, legally banned it. The majority of towns opted for warnings rather than court orders and bans. Mayor Jane Byrne of Chicago sent out one million leaflets about Halloween safety through schools, churches, libraries and human service organizations. Other towns invoked curfews, or limited the hours when children could trick or treat. Many communities resurrected the public community celebrations they'd held some 25 years before. Others offered candy coupons that adults could buy to pass out on Halloween and children could redeem the next day at a local store.

Many decried the hysteria that followed the Tylenol murders. Brian Sutton-Smith, writing in *Parents' Magazine* on Halloween 1983, said: "These holiday celebrations are our final resting places for trust and security. We cannot give them up and close our door, turn out our lights and snuff out the candles. The heart and future of our nation depends on their continuance."[4]

Public perception perhaps did not fairly represent the risk of Halloween trick or treating. A survey by sociologist Joel Best at California State University in Fresno found that in nearly 30 years (1958 to 1987), not a single death or severe injury was caused by a Halloween sadist.[5] Tamperings and copycat incidents numbered less than a dozen in all of New England, and only five to seven per major city (New York was unusual with 30 instances in one year).[6] Best found that tampering incidents were more likely to be fabricated by the children themselves or to be a smokescreen for other unrelated crimes. In *Editor and Publisher* (the newspaper industry's trade magazine), a report of newspapers' efforts to trace incidents of Halloween sadism concluded that nearly all were hoaxes. Yet the Halloween hysteria exists today, and the specter of Halloween tampering has taken a sobering place alongside other more friendly symbols of the celebration.[7]

Charity Remembered

People once gave food to the poor on behalf of dead souls on Halloween. The holiday's charitable function, old as its Christian roots, was lost with the Victorian era, but reassociated with Halloween in the 1940s.

With the ending of World War II, something seemed to stir in the American conscience. The public had seen what conventional warfare had done to Europe and what atomic warfare had done to Japan. And just as each member of the community helped out in the war effort, each was now urged to help in the world peace efforts that followed. Both the townwide Halloween events of the 1940s and '50s and the phenomenon of trick or treating were perfect vehicles for this. They were organized, they involved great numbers of people, and they were already associated with giveaways.

After the war, for example, children in Milwaukee charged a bar of soap as admission to their high school Halloween dance; the soap went to an orphanage in Freising, Germany. Trick-or-treaters in Palo Alto, California, gave up their candy in 1947 and instead solicited buttons, needles, pins, threads, snaps, shoelaces, elastic and thimbles for the American Friends Service Committee for distribution in Europe and Asia. Then, in 1950, a few children from a Philadelphia area Sunday school class sent UNICEF—the United Nations Children's Fund—the $17 they had collected trick or treating. UNICEF was an ideal recipient for Halloween charity. It had been created in 1946 to bring food, clothing and blankets to children who needed help after World War II, and was involved in the 1950s in a drive to get powdered milk to children of developing nations. The "Trick Or Treat for UNICEF" project was born right then and there and exists to this day.

This first small donation captured the hearts of a nation that genuinely wanted to help. Civic, religious and educational leaders encouraged children to collect money door to door for UNICEF on Halloween, and

Trick or Treat for UNICEF!
Children from Hawaii to Maine
collect money for UNICEF each
year on Halloween. (Photo cour-
tesy of UNICEF)

In recent decades Halloween has once more become a holiday for adults. One of the country's most popular city-wide Halloween parties is the annual Fantasy Festival held in Key West, Florida. (Photo courtesy Florida Department of Commerce, Division of Tourism)

helped out by giving UNICEF parties for them afterwards. On October 27, 1967, President Johnson proclaimed October 31 National UNICEF Day in the United States. By the 1970s, over three million American children in 13,000 communities were involved. And in the 37 years from 1950 to 1987, children have raised $83 million for UNICEF. Even in the 1980s, with concern over trick or treat, communities are encouraged to sponsor dances and carnivals to raise money to provide aid to children throughout the world.

Costumes, Masks and Halloween Trappings

Perhaps the most important part of a Halloween fete is the foolproof disguise. Some revelers opt for the traditional, and dress themselves as ghosts, witches, vampires, werewolves or any of a variety of ghouls and goblins. Others choose parody, donning likenesses of political leaders or movie stars. Still others look to history or mythology for inspiration, and some to objects of modern culture. For instance, children's costumes in the 1920s reflected the public's idols and interests; there were Topsys, Chinamen, Pierrots, clowns, Charlie Chaplins, cowboys, Indians, and the ubiquitous hobo. By the 1950s, children's costumes reflected the images made popular for each sex by an increasingly powerful media: witness the number of little princesses, brides and angels among girls; the army men and hoboes among boys. And television and movies have introduced a whole new cast of potential Halloween characters. According to veteran author and mother Teresa Bloomingdale, "I have outfitted athletes, angels, astronauts, firemen, Flintstones, monsters, Muppets, Mouseketeers, movie stars, rock stars and on one occasion, a Pet Rock."[8] During the peak of the *Star Wars* movies, Darth Vaders wandered the streets en masse; after the release of *E.T.* came the extraterrestrials. Halloween costuming in America had come of age and, along with it, Halloween marketing and industry.

At first the whole business of Halloween catered to children. "Free Weeny Witch Masks and a Party Book" were advertised with the purchase of Skinless Franks in the 1950s; "how to" Halloween books for children came out with recipes featuring the author's products, and foods were advertised as potential delights for trick-or-treaters. However, beginning in the 1970s, Halloween marketing shifted toward adults, and Halloween symbols sold products unrelated to Halloween. Vampires were used to sell cars and stereos, pumpkins lined the borders of print ads for records and tapes and spooky synthesized voices sold appliances over the radio. Like Washington's Birthday and the Fourth of July, Halloween was becoming an annual retail season in American advertising. This surge in Halloween merchandising closely followed the American adult's rediscovery of Halloween.

According to National Theme Productions, one of every four adults aged 18 to 40 wore a costume in 1980. By 1986, 60 percent of National Theme's Halloween costume rentals were to adults, and they sold three to five times more costumes than ever before. The Philadelphia Costume Company reported adults waiting in lines a block long for costumes that would cost them as much as $150 each.

Adults were just as influenced by the media as kids. In a Los Angeles costume shop, two media fantasy costumes outdid all others in rentals in 1980: futuristic knock-off costumes from the popular movie *Mad Max* and—on the other side of the spectrum—any costume from *Amadeus*, a Milos Forman movie based on the life of Mozart. In 1986, the *Wall Street Journal* reported four national favorites: the Ninja science-fiction character for men, a French courtesan for women, any vegetable and entertainer Tina Turner (either sex). The Western Costume Company in Hollywood, California, usually rents 4,000 costumes each year; according to its president, "...the gorilla costumes go first."

Halloween's popularity among America's adults is not new, but the adult frenzy for Halloween costumes and masks has never known such a wide scale. R. Chris Martin of the University of Missouri at Kansas City explains Halloween's current popularity with adults: it is a perfect "yuppie" holiday. The young urban professional finds Halloween a perfect fit with his life-style: "Instead of a Mercedes, he drives a BMW; instead of Chivas Regal, wine coolers; instead of a big family thing at Thanksgiving, Halloween, which has more flair and more style..."[9] Researchers at Hallmark—national distributors of much of the holiday's cards and party goods—attribute adult interest in Halloween to a current fascination with fantasy and trendy punk fashion and to the decreasing number of trick-or-treaters. There are also several other possibilities.

Unlike family celebrations such as Christmas or Thanksgiving, Halloween can be celebrated anywhere, and requires no trek homeward for independent adults. It is also one of the very few holidays that can be enjoyed equally by adults (singles or couples) and children. Halloween is the night when hardworking, responsible businesspeople can dress up as clowns, prisoners, presidents, strippers and vegetables; there is a freedom there found in no other holiday. Most of all, Halloween's current popularity may have something to do with nostalgia. The majority of adult celebrants remember the glory days of neighborhood trick or treating. Why not try to recreate the magic and freedom of a costume and mask on a pitch-black night?

Halloween Pageantry

Halloween and masquerades have gone hand in hand since medieval times. Parades of ghoulish characters drove the spirits from the villages of old Europe and parades of disguised townspeople begged house to house down through to the modern age. Costumed parades became part of American public celebrations in the 20th century, enjoyed on Thanksgiving, the Fourth of July and Easter as well as on Halloween. Although there are fewer costumed parades today, the ones that do exist are truly glorious tributes to the age-old spirit of community and grotesquerie.

Nowhere is this more obvious today than in one of America's grandest Halloween masquerades, the Greenwich Village Halloween parade. Hundreds of thousands of people gather on New York's Seventh Avenue at dusk to watch a stream of marchers sporting everything from bat wings to fuzzy dice. Pagan icons are reflected in the glass and mortar of modern-day Manhattan—a bulky, satyrlike figure with masterful horns and hollowed-out eyes, a great webbed creature with eyes of fire, witches, mice, devils, gods and ghouls. There are more modern images, too, like a full-sized washer and dryer set, a row of teeth and a group of screaming Japanese running from a paper-and-glue Godzilla.

The Greenwich Village parade is unusual among contemporary Halloween celebrations because it is one of the few large-scale celebrations that has not yet become a commercial venture. There are no prizes awarded, no corporate sponsorship, no grandstands printed with the names of local merchants. People come from all over the country to march in one of the nation's most outrageous, freewheeling costume extravaganzas simply for the joy of being there. "It is a night of inversion," says Jeanne Fleming, the parade's coordinator since 1980, "a night when good is turned inside out. The most famous person is not famous in a mask." Conversely, anybody can be famous on this one night.

The parade began in the early 1970s as a living exhibition of theater artist Ralph Lee's grotesque masks. Lee dressed up his children and friends on Halloween and paraded to Washington Square Park to put on a performance. New Yorkers loved the raggle-taggle troupe instantly. The next year the group grew larger, and by its eighth year the parade had gotten so large—150,000 people—that Ralph's figures cold no longer be seen among the crowds and he lost interest in the project. Jeanne Fleming then took it on.

Fleming, an artist specializing in large-scale outdoor theater pieces, found the Greenwich Village Halloween parade an exhilarating artistic challenge. She organized the parade as a nonprofit arts organization dedicated to street theater, puppetry and public performance and raised $40,000 to manage the event. She had barriers erected along the parade route to control the crowds, hired police and made sure the parade started and finished on time. She instituted programs in the schools, commissioned artists to build giant creatures and coordinated the media (seven to eight networks usually cover the parade; 12 to 14 foreign countries send film crews). Thanks to her efforts and to the truly celebratory nature of the event, the Greenwich Village Halloween parade attracts nearly 100,000 marchers and 250,000 spectators annually.

In the true spirit of inversion, satire abounds. In 1986, 49 schoolteachers marched as Imelda Marcos's shoes. 1986 was also the year pit bulls made the papers and the parade saw a conglomerate of glowering dogs masquerading as "Gladys Knight and the Pits." In 1987, a great goat god marched nearly nude down Seventh Avenue followed by Tina Turners, stockbrokers and a phalanx of female impersonators.

The impetus for the Halloween parade in New York still seems to come from the same sense of celebration that powered the old rituals—it is the last hurrah before the onset of dreary winter. "People need it to vent creativity, joy, energy, or they'll blow up," says Fleming. "It's the last fling before the long, cold winter. And it's a way of celebrating ancient Halloween rather than a modern, commercial one...just imagine the primitive images of the sweepers—old hags on stilts who begin the parade by sweeping up all the bad spirits and clearing a way for the marchers— silhouetted against the World Trade Center."

Ghosts, Witchcraft and the Ancestral Dead

Times change. Specters once ventured forth only on Halloween; now they come and go with any approaching darkness. Ancient ghosts embodied the wisdom and watchful eye of the ancestral dead; contemporary ghosts

ETHEREAL DISTURBANCES

According to a 1978 Gallup poll, only 11 percent of 1,500 people inter-viewed said they believed in ghosts. That was fewer than the number who believed in either Big Foot or the Loch Ness monster, and only slightly more than the number who believed in witches.

"When you talk of a ghost, there is ridicule," said Dr. Karlis Osis of the psychical research group, and although people may say they don't believe in ghosts, most wouldn't want to buy a house reputed to be haunted. "The value of the real-estate goes down," Dr. Osis said. He estimated that about four million people a year experience some type of ethereal disturbance.

—from the New York Times, *October 30, 1986*

seem to be avengers, malcontents, fortune-finders or simply confused and unable to find their way to the next world. Perhaps it was the loss of ancient Halloween that has disoriented them, leaving them shapeless vapor, unable to mark the progression of time with a fixed, annual celebration of death. Perhaps it is the notion that people no longer care enough to lay out groaning boards of food and wine on the night of All Hallows. Perhaps it's more that people move their families so often and so far that their ancestral dead simply cannot find them, and vice versa.

Contemporary life-styles call for a different relationship with the dead than that which formed the basis of Halloween so long ago. Ghost stories and reports of ghosts still abound, but Halloween is only one of the many occasions on which they're recounted. And reports of the ancestral dead returning to celebrate with the living are relatively few. Most contemporary ghost stories pit a new home owner or trespasser against the leftover ghost of the previous owner.

Whereas fascination with the spirit world at large (in the form of grotesque costuming, haunted houses, psychic fairs and the like) is very much a part of contemporary Halloween, concern with the ancestral dead is now exclusively the domain of religion. Catholics and Episcopalians across the country still gather together to pray for the departed on All Saints' and All Souls' Days. Mexican-Americans still visit the graves of their relatives to share food and wine on the Day of the Dead. And modern American witches observe Samhain—the original Halloween festival—in a tradition similar to that of the ancient Celts.

The renaissance of a ribald and exuberant adult celebration of Halloween ironically coincided with a quieter renaissance of witchcraft in America. Since the 1960s, a movement toward pagan religions has developed among those looking to make a connection with the rituals, symbols and myths of an ancient past. Although religious differences and history separate these neo-Pagans into sects (just as religious differences separated Protestants into many denominations), they share some common beliefs.

Nearly all neo-Pagans celebrate Beltane and Samhain as the two great festivals of the year. Samhain is spent in private or small group communion with one's ancestors. Often, food and wine are left as offerings to the dead. As it was for the Druids, this contemporary Samhain is a New Year's Eve celebration. Its rituals celebrate the worlds of both the dead and the living, the journey from darkness into light and death as a renewal of life. This philosophical and ritual celebration of Halloween stands as the sole survivor of an old-world pagan Halloween—the closest to Halloween in its original form.

WHY DO THEY RETURN?

According to Felix J. Cuervo, president of the Native New Yorker's Historical Association, ghosts return for a host of good reasons. His research for the Association's annual Halloween tour of New York's churchyards, buildings and gravesites has unearthed the following:

—Peter Stuyvesant, the last Dutch governor of New Amsterdam, returns to St. Mark's to try and ring the church bell. "They sometimes find a cord on the floor," says Cuervo.

—Humphrey Bogart returns to his childhood home on West 103rd Street to warn, "Don't stick around California too long."

—Aaron Burr walks the sea wall in the Battery looking for his daughter, Theodosia.

—Johnny Van Arsdale climbs a flagpole in the Battery to remind us of Evacuation Day, 1783. British soldiers had greased the pole, but Johnny nailed cleats to it and climbed it to hang an American flag.

—Lady Cornbury, Governor Edward Hyde's wife, returns to Trinity Churchyard apparently looking for interesting items to take. She had a reputation as a kleptomaniac and people usually hid things before she came to visit.

—Adam Allyn comes back to laugh. His gravestone in Trinity Churchyard is chiseled with the word, "Comedian."

—British actor George Frederick Cooke comes back to St. Paul's Churchyard, looking for his head. He was indigent at his death and couldn't pay the doctor. Cooke offered his head to science as payment; the doctor accepted. The head was used in several stage productions of Hamlet and is now at Jefferson Medical College in Pennsylvania.

—British soldiers return to City Hall Park and still try to chop down Liberty poles set up by rebels during the American Revolution.

Dread Lord of Shadows, God of Life and Bringer of Death. Yet as the knowledge of thee is Death, Open wide, I pray thee, thy gates through all must pass. Let our dear ones, who have gone before, return this night to make merry with us. And when our time comes, as it must, O' Thou, the Comforter and Consoler, the Giver of Peace and Rest, we will enter Thy realm gladly and unafraid. For we know that when rested and refreshed among our dear ones, we will be reborn again by thy grace and that of Lady Arida. Let it be the same place and same time as our dear ones, that we may love again.

—Prayer for Samhain from Jessie Wicker Bell, The Grimoire of Lady Sheba, *Llewellyn Publications, St. Paul, 1974.*

Celebrating Coast to Coast

The range of Halloween celebrations that exists in America today has produced a holiday full of dichotomy: it is a holiday for children, and for adults as well; a private day of religious observance and a day of public exhibition; a day for imaginative interpretation through costume and mask and a day for mass marketing; a day for conjuring up the spirit world in a society that has largely lost touch with the spirits of its own ancestral dead. And all across the country and in every state there are brand new Halloween traditions being born each year.

Each year at Boston College, a Romanian professor with an uncanny resemblance to the handsome Count Dracula of the 1400s masquerades as Vladimir Dracula for charity.

Nearby, in Salem, Massachusetts—a quiet harbor town known mostly for its shipping industry and, associated of course, with the hanging of 20 innocent people believed to be witches in 1692 (the crimes were committed in nearby Danvers, but Salem has somehow claimed the stigma), an annual "Haunted Happenings" celebration includes a Psychic Festival in the Old Town Hall, a Pumpkin Patch ham-and-bean supper and lectures sponsored by the Witches' League for Public Awareness.

Slightly south along the seaboard, the lights of Manhattan beckon celebrants of all sorts. St. Ann and the Holy Trinity Church has been known to give a concert composed of "Halloween Chambers of Horror Music." And small bands of brave souls take tours through Trinity Churchyard, the Battery and Washington Square which—unlikely as it seems now—was once a potter's field. This is a Native New Yorker Historical Society Association tour of real natives, New Yorkers who claimed their own six feet of earth a long time ago. And New York's Botanical Gardens are decorated each year with scenes of horror, such as Frankenstein and his bride cutting a petrified wedding cake.

In Baltimore, actors present the poems of Edgar Allan Poe by candlelight at his gravesite. And in Georgetown, there's an annual Halloween bash that serves as Washington, D.C.'s one-day version of Mardi Gras. Crowds of 100,000 people dressed as demons, ghouls and politicians fill the streets—even police dress in Halloween costume. Also in Washington, there's the unique black-tie Black Magic Ball—a salute to Harry Houdini, who died on Halloween and who many believe will send a message back to this world on this spooky anniversary.

Down South, the nocturnal world of bats is open to those who dare at the Atlanta Zoo. And in Garland, Texas, there's a Christian Halloween Carnival complete with a cakewalk. A radio broadcast from Boulder, Colorado, recreates the 1938 broadcast of "War of the Worlds"—just real enough to give an inkling of the thrill people would get meeting real visitors from another world, and just real enough to get a few phone calls from Boulder residents asking about shelters.

On the West coast sits the world's largest "pumpkin"—an 86,000 gallon Unocal tank painted orange and lit up for Halloween. And at the Erotic Exotic Ball in San Francisco, close to 10,000 brilliantly costumed celebrants dance well into the night to raise money for charity.

*   *   *

Today Halloween is a fixture of American culture, a beloved national holiday. But if the soul of Halloween—its connection with the unpredictable and unseen world of the spirit—had not been carefully guarded in our culture from the very beginning, the holiday might well have been lost to us. Although Halloween has never received the official legal status of Thanksgiving or the Fourth of July, it is nevertheless a feature of our calendars and a date anticipated with great excitement and preparation. Despite its commercial trappings and other pitfalls of any fully modern holiday, Halloween provides something that is unique: a full-fledged celebration of fantasy. It is the one night of the year when all is overturned, when the natural order reverses itself. The dead walk, the glamorous grow horrific, the ordinary becomes extraordinary. Children rebel and adults kick up their heels and holler at the moon. It is a holiday of magic and mystery, and one, though a peculiar blending of culture and custom, that is uniquely American.

Notes

1. Diana Karter Appelbaum, *Thanksgiving: An American Holiday, An American History*, Facts On File, New York, 1984, p. 29.
2. William Gaines, "Trick or Treating Crime in Burbank," *Chicago Tribune*, September 24, 1972, Section 10, p. 3.
3. The attempts to ban or inhibit trick or treating were local and unorganized. So were the counter demonstrations. In Homewood Village, Illinois, the village hall was picketed three weeks before Halloween by pre-teens lobbying for trick-or-treat rights. They had a petition signed by 50 adults asking that Halloween be left intact. And in Forest Park, Illinois, the Youth Commission rejected interference with Halloween. The commission advises the village board on matters affecting young people and includes six teenagers with full votes.
4. Brian Sutton-Smith, "What Happened to Halloween," *Parents Magazine*, Volume 58, October 1983, p. 65.
5. Joel Best, "The Razor Blade in the Apple: The Social Construction of Urban Legends," *Social Problems*, Volume 32, No. 5, June 1985, pp. 448-499.
6. Jordan Lipka and Frank Giordanella, "The Right to Trick or Treat: Constitutional Implications of Halloween Ordinances," *Harvard Journal of Legislation*, Volume 20 (2), pp. 601-615.
7. Best poses the theory that the belief in Halloween sadism is directly related to a fear that children today are in danger. He cites the movement against child abuse, emerging campaigns against incest, child pornography and abortion as contributors to the sense of children being in jeopardy ("The Razor Blade in the Apple," p. 493).
8. Theresa Bloomingdale, "Tricks and Treats and Purloined Sheets," *McCall's*, October 1983, p. 74.
9. "Adults Spurring a Boom in Halloween," *New York Times*, October 31, 1986, p. D-1.

Bibliography

Margot Adler, *Drawing Down the Moon*, Beacon Press, Boston, 1979.

"Adults Spurring a Boom in Halloween," *New York Times*, October 31, 1986.

A.G.T., "All-Hallowe'en," *Godey's Lady's Book*, Volume 97, October 1878.

Margaret Ainslee, "Hints for Hallowe'en Hilarities," *Ladies' Home Journal*, Volume 27, October 1910

Catherine Harris Ainsworth, "Halloween," *New York Folklore Quarterly*, Volume 29, September 1973.

"Air Wardens Will Help Curb Halloween Vandals," *New York Times*, October 29, 1942.

John W. Allen, *It Happened in Southern Illinois*, Southern Illinois University Press, Carbondale, 1973.

"All-Hallowe'en," *Godey's Lady's Book*, Volume 109, October 1884.

John Q. Anderson, "The Legend of the Phantom Coach of East Texas," *Western Folklore*, Volume 22, Number 4, 1963.

Diana Karter Applebaum, *Thanksgiving: An American Holiday, An American History*, Facts On File, New York, 1984.

Margerite Aspinwall, "A Halloween Maypole," *Woman's Home Companion*, Volume 27, October 1925.

Edna Barth, *Witches, Pumpkins and Grinning Ghosts: The Story of the Halloween Symbols*, Seabury Press, New York, 1963.

Lina Beard, "Witchery Games for Halloween," *The Delineator*, Volume 64, October 1904.

———, "Halloween Fortunes for Boys and Girls," *The Delineator*, Volume 66, October 1905.

Lina Beard and Adelia G. Beard, *The American Girl's Handy Book*, Charles E. Tuttle Company, Rutland, Vermont, 1969.

Horace P. Beck, *The Folklore of Maine*, J. B. Lippincott Company, Philadelphia, 1957.

Jessie Wicker Bell, *The Grimoire of Lady Sheba*, Llewellyn Publications, St. Paul, Minnesota, 1974.

Joel Benton, "Hallowe'en," *Harper's Weekly*, Volume 39, December 7, 1895.

———, "Hallowe'en," *The Outlook*, October 27, 1900.

Joel Best and Gerald Horiuchi, "The Razor Blade in the Apple: The Social Construction of Urban Legends," *Social Problems*, Volume 32, June 1985.

Henry Bett, *The Games of Children*, reissued by Singing Tree Press, Detroit, Michigan, 1968.

Elizabeth F. Bingham, "The Tryst of the Witches," *Good Housekeeping*, Volume 53, October 1911.

Mary E. Blain, *Games for All Occasions*, Barse and Hopkins, Brewer, Barse & Company, New York, 1909.

Teresa Bloomingdale, "Tricks and Treats and Purloined Sheets," *McCall's*, Volume 111, October 1983.

B. A. Botkin, editor, *A Treasury of American Folklore*, Crown Publishers, New York, 1944.

_____, *A Treasury of New England Folklore*, Crown Publishers, New York, 1947.

_____, *A Treasury of Southern Folklore*, Crown Publishers, New York, 1949.

Sarah Guernsey Bradley, "The Different Party," *Harper's Bazar*, Volume 41, February 1907.

R. Brasch, *How Did It Begin?* David McKay Company, New York, 1965.

Ebenezer Cobham Brewer, *Dictionary of Phrase and Fable*, Harper & Row Publishers, New York, 1965.

Adrienne Brugard, "The Revel of the Witches," *The Delineator*, Volume 78, October 1911.

Jan Harold Brunvand, editor, *Readings in American Folklore*, W. W. Norton & Co., Inc., New York, 1979.

Robert Burns, *The Complete Poetical Works of Burns*, Cambridge edition, Houghton Mifflin Company, Boston, 1897.

Patricia Burton, "Festival Time at Halloween," *Recreation*, Volume 49, September 1956.

Jon Butler, "Magic, Astrology and the Early American Religious Heritage 1600–1760," *American Historical Review*, Volume 84, April 1979.

Thaddeus J. Butler, *The Catholic Church in America*, W. B. Kelly, Dublin, 1869.

Hezekiah Butterworth, "Captain Tuttle's Magic Clock," *In Old New England: The Romance of a Colonial Fireside*, D. Appleton & Co., New York, 1895.

"Byrne Urges Extra Caution by Parents for Halloween," *Chicago Tribune*, October 20, 1982.

"'Candy Man' Who Killed Son Has Date With Death," *Chicago Tribune*, October 25, 1982.

"Careful Planning Pays," *Recreation*, Volume 49, September 1956.

George G. Carey, *A Faraway Time and Place: Lore of the Eastern Shore*, Robert B. Luce, Inc., New York, 1971.

―――, *Maryland Folklore and Folklife*, Tidewater Publishers, Cambridge, Massachusetts, 1970.

"Caught in the Act of Growing Up," *Chicago Tribune*, October 31, 1987.

A Celebration of American Family Folklife, Collected for the Family Folklife Program of the Smithsonian's Festival of American Folklife, Pantheon, New York, 1982.

"Celebration Postponed to Nov. 2, Hagerstown, Maryland," *New York Times*, August 23, 1936.

"Chasing the Hallowe'en Goblins," *Educational Review*, October 1927.

"Chicago City Council Votes Observance Abolition for War Duration," *New York Times*, October 15, 1942.

Ella Rodman Church, "Through a Looking-Glass," *Godey's Lady's Book*, Volume 101, October 1880.

Joseph D. Clark, "All Saints' Day and Halloween," *North Carolina Folklore*, Volume 20, Number 3, 1972.

Tristram P. Coffin and Hennig Cohen, editors, *Folklore in America*, selected from the *Journal of American Folklore*, Doubleday & Co., Inc., New York, 1966.

Tristram P. Coffin and Hennig Cohen, editors, *Folklore From the Working Folk of America*, Anchor Press/Doubleday, New York, 1973.

David Steven Cohen, *The Ramapo Mountain People*, Rutgers University Press, New Jersey, 1974.

"Community-wide Halloween Planning Establishing New Customs," *Recreation*, Volume 46, September 1952.

Mary Caroline Crawford, *Social Life in Old New England*, Little, Brown & Co., Boston, 1914.

"Crowd Sees Woman Pray," *New York Times*, November 3, 1923.

Mary Curran, "Halloween for the Whole Town," *The Delineator*, Volume 99, November 1921.

Isabel Gordon Curtis, "A Children's Celebration of Halloween," *St. Nicholas Magazine*, Volume 32, Part II, October 1905.

Leslie Daiken, *Children's Games Throughout the Year*, B. T. Batsford, Ltd., London, 1949.

Mary Dawson, "Entertain Your Guests with Ghosts, Sorcery and the Black Arts. They'll Like It," *The Delineator*, Volume 83, November 1913.

Linda Degh, editor, *Indiana Folklore*, Indiana University Press, Indiana, 1980.

Claudia de Lys, *A Treasury of American Superstitions*, Philosophical Library, New York, 1968.

"Detroit Takes Steps for Sane Halloween," *New York Times*, October 27, 1935.

Edward Diener, Arthur L. Beaman, Scott C. Fraser and Roger T. Kelem, "Effects of Deindividuation Variable on Stealing Among Halloween Trick or Treaters," *Journal of Personality and Social Psychology*, Volume 33, Number 2, 1976.

Richard M. Dorson, *America In Legend: Folklore from the Colonial Period to the Present*, Pantheon Books, New York, 1973.

George William Douglas, *The American Book of Days*, revised by Helen Douglas Compton, H. W. Wilson Company, New York, 1948.

Samuel Adams Drake, *A Book of New England Legends and Folklore*, Roberts Brothers, Boston, 1884.

———, *The Myths and Fables of To-day*, Lee & Shepard, Boston, 1900.

"The Dumb Cake: A Charm of Hallowe'en," *Godey's Lady's Book*, Volume 91, October 1875.

Letitia Virginia Douglas, "The Face in the Glass: A Halloween Sketch," *Godey's Lady's Book*, Volume 123, October 1891.

Alice Morse Earle, *Colonial Dames and Goodwives*, Frederick Unger Publishing Co., New York, 1962.

———, *Colonial Days in Old New York*, Charles Scribner & Sons, New York, 1896.

———, *Customs and Fashions in Old New England*, Charles Scribner & Sons, New York, 1893.

———, *In Old Narragansett/Romances and Realities*, Charles Scribner & Sons, New York, 1898.

Lina Eckenstein, *Comparative Studies in Nursery Rhymes*, Singing Tree Press, Detroit, Michigan, 1968.

Mircea Eliade, *A History of Religious Ideas*, University of Chicago Press, Chicago, 1978.

Ellen Elliot, "Hallowe'en," *Godey's Lady's Book*, Volume 81, October 1870.

Gabrielle Elliot and Arthur R. Forbush, *Games for Every Day*, Macmillan Company, New York, 1926.

Marion Vallat Emrick and George Korson, editors, *The Child's Book of Folklore*, Dial Press, New York, 1947.

"EP Curran Warns Against Auto Damage," *New York Times*, October 27, 1937.

"Episcopal Church Will Conduct Special Service Next Tuesday," *Atlanta Constitution*, October 31, 1895.

Sara Evans, "The New Halloween," *Parent's Magazine*, Volume 58, October 1983.

Vergilus Ferm, *A Brief Dictionary of American Superstition*, Philosophical Library, New York, 1959.

"50 New Rochelle Boys Act as Halloween Police," *New York Times*, November 1, 1923.

"Fires and Firemen," *New York Times*, October 26, 1986.

Sir James George Frazer, *The New Golden Bough*, Dr. Theodore H. Gaster, editor, Criterion Books, New York, 1959.

S. Annie Frost, "Hallowe'en at Farmdale," *Godey's Lady's Book*, Volume 87, September 1873.

"Fun for Hallowe'en," *Ladies' Home Journal*, Volume 124, October 1907.

"Games for Halloween," *Boston Globe*, October 31, 1900.

William Gaines, "Trick or Treating Crime in Burbank," *Chicago Tribune*, September 24, 1972.

Emelyn Elizabeth Gardner, *Folklore From the Schoharie Hills New York*, Arno Press, New York, 1977.

Henry Glassie, *Pattern in the Material Folk Culture of the Eastern U.S.*, University of Pennsylvania Press, Philadelphia, 1968.

"The Goblins Will Getcha," *Newsweek*, November 3, 1975.

Ruby Ross Goodnow, "Entertainment in October," *The Delineator*, Volume 78, October 1911.

Mrs. Moody P. Gore and Mrs. Guy Speare, *New Hampshire Folk Tales*, New Hampshire Federation of Women's Clubs, Plymouth, New Hampshire, 1932.

John Greenway, *Folklore of the Great West*, American West Publishing Company, Palo Alto, California, 1960.

"Hallowe'en," *Godey's Lady's Book*, Volume 85, October 1872.

"Halloween: A Pagan Festival," *Craftsman Magazine*, Volume 19, November 1910.

"Halloween Community Style," *Recreation*, Volume 37, October 1943.

"Halloween Damage Disappears with City Celebrations," *Recreation*, Volume 35, October 1941.

"Halloween Hoopla Is No Longer Just For Kids," *Wall Street Journal*, October 16, 1986.

"Halloween in the Parks," *New York Times*, October 30, 1941.

"The Hallowe'en Party," *Ladies' Home Journal*, Volume 30, October 1913.

"Halloween Scary Story Contest," *Denver Post*, October 31, 1987.

"Halloween Spirit Faithful to Past," *New York Times*, October 29, 1933.

"Halloween—Why Thousands Will Think of Erin Tonight," *Boston Daily Globe*, October 31, 1884.

Darlene Hamilton, *Resources for Creative Teaching in Early Childhood Education*, Harcourt Brace Jovanovich, New York, 1977.

Edith Hamilton, *Mythology*, New American Library, New York, 1969.

Florence Hamsher, *The Complete Book of Children's Parties*, Doubleday & Co., New York, 1949.

Wayland D. Hand, "European Fairy Lore in the New World," *Folklore*, Volume 92, 1981.

Wayland D. Hand, editor, *The Frank C. Brown Collection of North Carolina Folklore, Popular Beliefs and Superstitions from North Carolina*, Volumes VI and VII, Duke University Press, Durham, North Carolina, 1961.

E. V. Harbin, *The Fun Encyclopedia*, Abingdon-Cokesbury Press, New York, 1940.

Jean Harrowven, *The Origins of Rhymes, Songs & Sayings*, Kaye & Ward, London, 1977.

Estelle M. Hart, "A Real Halloween," *The House Beautiful*, October 1916.

Bertha Hasbrook, "A Nut-Crack Night Party," *Harper's Bazar*, Volume 41, November 1907.

Jane M. Hatch, editor, *American Book of Days*, 3rd edition, H. W. Wilson, New York, 1978.

Star Hawk, *The Spiral Dance*, Harper & Row Publishers, New York, 1979.

"Hempstead Police Investigate Stone-Throwing and Other Depredations," *New York Times*, November 2, 1923.

"Hits Halloween Revels," *New York Times*, October 23, 1942, p. 16.

Alice Crowell Hoffman, "Games for Halloween," *Parents' Magazine*, Volume 6, October 1931.

Christina Hole, *English Traditional Customs*, Rowman & Littlefield, Totowa, New Jersey, 1975.

Wayman Hogue, *Back Yonder: An Ozark Chronicle*, Minton, Balch & Co., New York, 1932.

Hanz Holzer, *Ghosts of the Golden West*, Bobbs-Merrill Company, Indianapolis, 1968.

Kate Hopkins, "The Hallowe'en Witch Party," *Harper's Bazar*, Volume 39, November 1905.

"How One City Handles Halloween," *Recreation*, Volume 44, September 1950.

Lois Phillips Hudson, "The Buggy on the Roof," *Atlantic Monthly*, Volume 210, November 1962.

Eleanor Hull, *Folklore of the British Isles*, Methuen & Company, Ltd., London, 1928.

Harry Middleton Hyatt, *Folklore From Adams County Illinois*, Memoirs of the Alma Egan Hyatt Foundation, New York, 1935.

Marguerite Ickis, *A Book of Festival Holidays*, Dodd, Mead & Co., New York, 1964.

——, *The Book of Games and Entertainment the World Over*, Dodd, Mead & Co., New York, 1969.

Clifton Johnson, *What They Say in New England*, Lee & Shepard, Boston, 1895.

F. Roy Johnson, *Legends and Myths of North Carolina Roanoke-Chowan Area*, Johnson Publishing Company, Murfreesboro, North Carolina, 1971.

June Johnson, *The Outdoor-Indoor Fun Book*, Gramercy Publishing Co., New York, 1961.

"A Jolly Good Time for Hallowe'en," *The Delineator*, Volume 74, October 1909.

Mildred Jordan, *The Distelfink Country of the Pennsylvania Dutch*, Crown Publishers, New York, 1978.

Saul Kaplan, "Halloween, Then," *New York Times*, October 28, 1987.

"Kid's Day Is Offering New Halloween Haunts," *Chicago Tribune*, October 30, 1986.

Elsie Kingdom, "Hallowe'en Supper," *Harper's Bazar*, Volume 37, November 1903.

Mrs. Burton Kingsland, *In and Outdoor Games*, Doubleday Page & Co., New York, 1904.

Mary and Herbert Knapp, *One Potato, Two Potato*, W. W. Norton & Co., New York, 1976.

T. Sharpe Knowlson, *The Origins of Popular Superstitions, Customs & Ceremonies*, T. Werner Laurie, London, 1910.

David Thomas Konig, *Law and Society in Puritan Massachusetts: Essex County, 1629–1692*, University of North Carolina Press, Chapel Hill, 1973.

Maymie R. Krythe, *All About American Holidays*, Harper & Row Publishers, New York, 1962.

Oscar Kuhns, *The German and Swiss Settlements of Colonial Pennsylvania: A Study of the So-Called Pennsylvania Dutch*, Henry Holt & Co., New York, 1901.

Thomas H. Kunz, "Halloween Treat—Bat Facts and Folklore," *American Biology Teacher*, Volume 46, Number 7, 1984.

"Lads and Lassies, All Halloween Is Here," *Atlanta Constitution*, October 31, 1897.

Robert Lasson and David Eynon, "Just Say Trick-or-Treat-O-Mat," *McCall's*, Volume 95, October 1967.

Anatole LeBraz, "All Souls' Eve in Lower Brittany," *The Living Age*, The Living Age Co., Number 2745, February 13, 1897.

"Legends and Superstitions," *St. Nicholas Magazine*, Volume 3, November 1874.

Joe T. Leszcynski, R. B. McClintock, Beatrice Klughaupt and John Alexander, "Halloween Shenanigans—A Tale of Five Cities," *Recreation*, Volume 41, September 1947.

Mary Ellen Brown Lewis, "Folk Elements in Scotch-Irish Presbyterian Communities," *Pennsylvania Folklife*, Volume 18, 1968.

Nellie M. Lewis, *Games and Parties the Year Around*, Airment Books, New York, 1954.

Ralph and Adelin Linton, *Halloween Through 20 Centuries*, Henry Schuman, New York, 1950.

Jordan Lipka and Frank Giordanella, "The Right to Trick or Treat: Constitutional Implications of Halloween Ordinances," *Harvard Journal of Legislation*, Volume 20, 1983.

"Live Pigs Let Loose at Halloween Dance," *New York Times*, October 29, 1933.

Henry Wadsworth Longfellow, "The Song of Hiawatha," *The Poems of Longfellow*, Modern Library, New York, 1944.

William DeLoss Love Jr., *Fast and Thanksgiving Days*, Houghton Mifflin Company, Boston, 1895.

Mary McKim Marriott, "Social Affairs for Hallowe'en," *Ladies' Home Journal*, Volume 25, October 1908.

"Masked Balls," *Harper's Weekly*, February 6, 1875.

Bernard S. Mason and Elmer D. Mitchell, *Party Games,* Barnes & Noble, New York, 1947.

Nan L. Mildren, "A Halloween Entertainment for Rural Schools," *Ladies' Home Journal*, October 1913.

James F. McCloy and Ray Miller Jr., *The Jersey Devil*, Middle Atlantic Press, Wallingford, Pennsylvania, 1976.

Nancy McDonough, *Garden Sass: A Catalog of Arkansas Folklore*, Coward, McCann & Geoghegan, New York, 1975.

Carol McGraw, "Bewitching—Covens of the 80's Don't Match Lore Stirred by Tales of Halloweens Past," *Los Angeles Times*, October 31, 1987.

W. K. McNeil, editor, *Ghost Stories From the American South*, August House, Little Rock, Arkansas, 1985.

F. Marian McNeill, *Halloween Its Origins, Rites and Ceremonies in the Scottish Tradition*, Albyn Press, Edinburgh, 1970.

Margaret Mead, "Halloween: Where Has All the Mischief Gone?" *Redbook*, Volume 145, October 1975.

George Mendora, *Norman Rockwell's Happy Holidays*, G. P. Putnam's Sons, New York, 1983.

Nan L. Mildren, "A Halloween Entertainment for Rural Schools," *Ladies' Home Journal*, Volume 30, October 1913.

Marie Eulalie Moran, "Hallowe'en Fun," *Ladies' Home Journal*, Volume 23, October 1906.

Louise Morgan, "They Dared Great Things," *Mysterious New England*, Austin N. Stevens, editor, Yankee Publishing, Dublin, New Hampshire, 1971.

Mrs. Hamilton Mott, editor, *Home Games and Parties*, Ladies' Home Journal Girls' Library, Curtis Publishing Company, Philadelphia, 1891.

"Moves to Drop Halloween," *New York Times*, October 15, 1942.

Margaret E. Mulac, *The Game Book*, Harper & Brothers Publishers, New York and London, 1946.

Margaret E. Mulac and Marian S. Holmes, *The Party Game Book*, Harper & Brothers Publishers, New York, 1951.

Robert J. Myers, editor, *Celebrations: The Complete Book of American Holidays*, Doubleday & Co., New York, 1972.

Susanna Myers, *Folk-Songs of the Four Seasons*, G. Schirmer, New York, 1929.

National Halloween Committee of New York City, "Suggestions for Promoting Halloween Parties," *Recreation*, Volume 43, September 1949.

"A National Occasion for Merrymaking," *American City*, Volume 43, October 1930.

"New Britain Changes Its Plans," *Recreation*, Volume 37, October 1943.

"New Style Halloween in a Town in Kansas," *New York Times*, October 27, 1935.

"A Night for Ghosts, Real and Unreal," *New York Times*, October 30, 1986.

"A Night With the Master of Terror and We Don't Mean Stephen King," *Wall Street Journal*, October 31, 1986.

"No Halloween Rough Stuff, Mayor Warns," *New York Times*, October 31, 1942.

"Notes on Halloween," *Atlanta Constitution*, October 31, 1897.

G. F. Northall, *English Folk-Rhymes*, Kegan Paul, Trench, Trübner & Co., reissued by Singing Tree Press, Detroit, Michigan, 1968.

"A Novel Hallowe'en Party," *Harper's Bazar*, Volume 38, November 1904.

"1000 Windows in Queens Broken on Halloween," *New York Times*, November 1, 1939.

Iona and Peter Opie, *The Lore and Language of Schoolchildren*, Clarendon Press, Oxford, England, 1959.

Emma A. Opper, "The Charms," *Munsey's Magazine*, Volume 30, November 1903.

Roderick Peattie, editor, *The Great Smokies and the Blue Ridge*, Vanguard Press, New York, 1943.

Newbell Niles Puckett, *Folk Beliefs of the Southern Negro*, Dover Publications, New York, 1969.

Susan Gold Purdy, *Festivals for You to Celebrate*, J. B. Lippincott Company, Philadelphia, 1969.

Anna Quindlen, "Life in the 30's," *New York Times*, October 28, 1987.

E. and M. A. Radford, *Encyclopedia of Superstitions*, Philosophical Library, New York, 1949.

Vance Randolph, *Ozark Magic and Folklore*, Dover Publications, New York, 1964 (Second publishing; first was by Columbia University Press, 1947).

"Record Throng in Newark Sees Halloween Parade," *New York Times*, November 3, 1939.

"Reforming Halloween," *New York Times*, October 27, 1935

"A Review of Matters of the Moment," *Educational Review*, Volume 74, October 1927.

Adrienne Cecile Rich, "All Hallows' Eve," *New Yorker*, Volume 31, October 29, 1955.

Leonard W. Roberts, *South From Hell-fer-Sartin/Kentucky Mountain Tales*, Council of Southern Mountains, Berea, Kentucky, 1961.

"Roman Catholic Schools," *Harper's Weekly*, Volume 14, February 6, 1875.

Parke Rouse Jr., *Planters and Pioneers/Life in Colonial Virginia*, Hastings House, New York, 1968.

Ruth Virginia Sacket, "Entertainments for Halloween," *The Delineator*, Volume 64, October 1904.

Jack Santino, "Halloween in America," *Western Folklore*, Volume 42, Number 1, 1983.

"Satan Got a Lawyer in Arkansas," *Chicago Tribune*, November 30, 1986.

Alvin Schwartz, editor, *When I Grew Up Long Ago*, J. B. Lippincott Company, Philadelphia, 1978.

H. H. Scullard, *Festivals & Ceremonies of the Roman Republic*, Cornell University Press, Ithaca, New York, 1981.

Anna Wentworth Sears, "Games for Halloween," *Harper's Bazar*, Volume 33, October 27, 1900.

"Simply One More Holiday," *New York Times*, November 1, 1926.

Michael Small, "The Halloween Effect," *Psychology Today*, Volume 13, October 1979.

Brian Sutton Smith, "What Happened to Halloween," *Parents' Magazine*, Volume 58, October 1983.

Mrs. Guy E. Speare (compiler and publisher), *More New Hampshire Folk Tales*, Plymouth, New Hampshire, 1936.

Marion L. Starkey, *The Devil in Massachusetts*, Doubleday/Anchor, Garden City, New York, 1969.

Burton E. Stevenson and Elizabeth B. Stevenson, *Days and Deeds/Prose for Children's Reading and Speaking*, Doubleday Doran & Co., New York, 1941.

Gregory P. Stone, "Halloween and the Mass Child," *The American Culture*, Hennig Cohen, editor, Cambridge edition, Houghton Mifflin Company, Boston, 1897.

"Stores Bid Youth Soap Windows," *New York Times*, October 28, 1939.

Margaret Sweeney, *Fact, Fiction & Folklore of Southern Indiana*, Vantage Press, New York, 1967.

Laura Gates Sykora, "Halloween Merriment," *The Delineator*, Volume 95, October 1919.

Mae McGuire Telford, "What Shall We Do Hallowe'en?" *Ladies' Home Journal*, Volume 37, October 1920.

"They Scare Up Pennies," *Recreation*, Volume 58, October 1965.

Olive Thorne, "Witches Night," *St. Nicholas Magazine*, Volume 6, October 1879.

"To Make Halloween Safe and Sane," *The Survey*, Volume 39, October 6, 1917.

"To-Night is Hallowe'en," *Hartford Daily Courant*, October 31, 1895.

"To-Night Will be Hollowe'en [sic]," *Hartford Daily Courant*, October 31, 1885.

"Too Many Tricks, Treating Trimmed," *Chicago Tribune*, October 29, 1972.

Elizabeth Phipps Train, "The Hallow-e'en Sensation at Gov'ner Dering's," *Godey's Lady's Book*, Volume 117, October 1888.

"Trick or Treating Crime in Burbank," *Chicago Tribune*, September 24, 1972.

Victor Turner, editor, *Celebration Studies in Festivity and Ritual*, Smithsonian Institution Press, Washington, D.C., 1982.

Mark Twain, *The Adventures of Huckleberry Finn*, in *The Adventures of Huckleberry Finn, An Annotated Text, Backgrounds and Source Essays in Criticism*, Sculley Bradley, editor, W. W. Norton & Co., New York, 1961.

"Tylenol, Halloween and Hysteria," *Chicago Tribune*, October 27, 1982.

UPI, "Halloween No Longer Just For Children," *Hartford Daily Courant*, October 31, 1986.

Eunice Ware, "The Goblin's Phone on Halloween," *Recreation*, Volume 45, October 1951.

"War Recreation Congress," *Recreation*, Volume 36, October 1942.

Grace L. Weeks, "Merry Hallowe'en Larks," *Ladies' Home Journal*, Volume 20, October 1903.

Francis X. Weiser, *The Holyday Book*, Harcourt Brace, New York, 1956.

Amos R. Wells, *Social-To Save*, United Society of Christian Endeavor, Boston and Chicago, 1895.

Carolyn Wells, "A Nonsense Calendar," *St. Nicholas Magazine*, Volume 30, Part II, October 1901.

J. D. Wernhaner and R. Dodder, "A New Halloween Goblin: The Product Tamperings," *Journal of Popular Culture*, Volume 18, Winter 1984.

Ralph Whitlock, *A Calendar of Country Customs*, B. T. Batsford, London, 1978.

Annie Weston Whitney and Caroline Canfield Bullock (compilers), "Folklore from Maryland," *Memoirs of the American Folk-Lore Society*, Volume 18, 1925 (New York).

Francis P. Wightman, *Little Leather Breeches and Other Southern Rhymes*, J. F. Taylor & Co., New York, 1899.

Griffith Wilde, "By Cupid's Trick: A Parlor Drama for All Hallowe'en," *Godey's Lady's Book*, Volume 111, November 1885.

Henry T. Williams and S. Annie Frost, *Merry Hours for Merry People*, Volume V of *Williams' Household Series*, Henry T. Williams, Publisher, New York, 1878.

Edna Erle Wilson, "The Dixie Dance for All-Hallow Even," *The Delineator*, Volume 95, October 1919.

———, "Halloween, Occult and Shuddery," *The Delineator*, Volume 97, October 1920.

"Windows Bloom on Goblin Night," *Recreation*, Volume 44, October 1950.

Clement Wood and Gloria Goddard, *The Complete Book of Games*, Doubleday & Co., New York, 1940.

Ray Wood, *Fun in American Folk Rhymes*, J. B. Lippincott Company, Philadelphia, 1952.

Index

(Italic numbers indicate illustrations)

A

Adams, John 30
Advertising 149–150
Agricultural Revolution 21, 66
Allen, Frederick D. 30
Allentown, Pennsylvania 124
All Saints' Day
  Black Americans and 86
  Colonial America and 22
  Delaware and 45
  Early Christian celebration of 8–14
  Georgia and 47
  Irish celebration of 67
  in 20th Century 121
  Victorians and 104
All Souls' Bread Recipe 13
All Souls' Day
  Colonial America and 22
  Day of the Dead and 94
  Early Christian celebration of 8–14
  Georgia and 47
  Ireland and 67
  in 20th Century 121
All Souls' Night (poem) 57
Allyn, Adam 155
Amalarius 11
American Indians 19, 26
American Revolution 30, 51
Andrew, Saint 45
Anglicans 24
Anoka, Minnesota 121, *122–123*
Apocrypha (book) 11
Appalachia 80–83

Apple-Peeling 80, 113
Apples
  Celtic traditions and 56
  Colonial traditions and 63
  Festival of Samhain and 8
  Irish traditions and 72
  Roman traditions and 6–7, 57
  Victorian traditions and 108
April Fool's Day 27
Arizona 93
Arkansas 56
Arson 124–131
Astrology 23, 34, 43
Atlanta Constitution (newspaper) 111, 116

B

Baal (god) 62
Baltimore, Lord 45
Bangs, John Kendrick 61
Bannock, Tuggie 60
Baptists 38, 41
Bats 158
Beheading of the Ghost 134
Belcher, Governor 27
Ben, Gary 81–82
Berkeley, Edmund 23
Berrying the Ghost *118*
Best, Joel 145
Bible, The (book) 23, 113
Big Foot 153
Black Americans 86–87, 91–92—*See also*
  Slaves and Slavery
Black Cats 65, 88–90, 116, 119

Bloomingdale, Teresa 149
Bobbing for Apples *100*, 108, 113, 119
Bogart, Humphrey 155
Boniface IV, Pope 9
Boston, Massachusetts 129
Boston Daily Globe (newspaper) 104
Boulton, Robert 3
Bradford, William 28
Brujas 85, 93
Buck, Jonathan 37
Burns, Robert 101
Burr, Aaron 155
Butler, Jon 34
Butler, Samuel 78
Byrne, Jane 145

C
Cabbage 72
California 93
Calvin, John 14
Calvinists 14, 25, 34, 39
Carteret, George 41
Catesby, Robert 15
Cauchemar 88
Cave of the Devil, The 93
Celtic Tribes
   Apples and Nuts and 56
   Divination traditions of 71
   Early traditions 1
   Festival of Samhain 2–5
   Festival of Taman 6
   Southern states and 83
Chango (god) 85
Charles I, King (Great Britain) 25, 45
Charms, The (poem) *109*
Chernabog 5
Chicago Principals' Club 126
Chiromancy 23
Christianity 8–14—*See also specific de-
   nominations*
College Colors, Test of 115
Congregationalists 41
Connecticut 21, 25, 36–38
Constantine (Roman emperor) 8
Cooke, George Frederick 155
Cornbury, Lady 155
Corn Husking *55*

Coronado, California 135
Corpse Candles 78
Costumes 116–119, 149–151
Count Dracula—*See Dracula*
Cuervo, Felix J. 155
Culpeper, Nicholas 23
Cyanide Poisoning 143–146

D
Damballah (god) 85
Darth Vader (fictional character) 149
Darwin, Charles 99
David, Saint 45
Day of the Dead 26, 66, 94, 154
Delaware 44–45
Delineator, The (magazine) 124
Devil, a Beetle and a Bleeding Toe, The
   (story) 81
Devil in Massachusetts, The (book) 34
Dialect Notes (book) 30
Divination Traditions
   of Appalachia 80
   Apple Peel Throwing *74*
   of Ireland *69*, 76
   Kale-Pulling 80
   of Massachusetts Bay Colony 31, 34
   with Mirrors *73*, 75
   of Rhode Island 39
   of Southern States 92
   of Victorians 108–111, 113–116, 120
   of Virginia 23
   Vodoun and 86
   Yarn-Winding 80
Dracula, Count 157
Druids
   Divination traditions of 71
   Festival of Pomona 8
   Festival of Samhain 2, 65
   Festival of Taman 6
   Ghost stories and 59
   History of 1–2
Dumb Supper 75, 87, 108, 111

E
Editor and Publisher (magazine) 146
Election Day 25
Elizabeth I, Queen (England) 22, 25

England
  Divination games of 8
  Guy Fawkes Day 14–16
E.T. (film) 149
Evansville, Indiana 124

F

Fantasia (film) *5*
Fantasy Festival *148*
Fawkes, Guy 15
Fitzgerald, John W. 145
Flemming, Jeanne 151–152
Folk Beliefs of the Southern Negro (book)
  83
Forman, Milos 150
Fortune-Telling 23, 34, *106*, 120
Fort Wayne, Indiana 133
Fourth of July 63, 135, 158
Franciscans 47
Frazer, Dr. James George 59
Frost, A. B. 55

G

George, Saint 24, 45
George III, King (Great Britain) 15
Georgia 47, 56, 114
Germany 80–83
Ghosts 152–158
Ghosts, The (poem) *26*
Ghost Stories
  Colonial America and 57–61
  of Ireland *69*
  Play parties and 53
  Puritans and 39
  in the 20th Century 154
  Victorians and 107, 115
Glens Falls, New York 124
Godey's Lady's Book (magazine) 101, 107
Gose, Rindy Sue 81–82
Greenwich Village Halloween Parade 151
Gregory I, Pope 9
Gregory II, Pope 9
Gregory IV, Pope 9
Groliks 80
Guisers 44
Guising 44
Gunpowder Plot—*See Guy Fawkes Day*

Guy Fawkes Day
  Colonial America and 24, 27, 30, 36,
    39–40, 47, 56
  Ireland and 71
  Mischief Night and 61, 63
  Origin of 14–16
  Trick or treating and 142

H

Hagerstown, Maryland 124
Hallowe'en (poem) 101
Halloween (poem) 102
Halloween (poem by Bangs) 61
Halloween in Colonial Days (drawing)
  20
*Hallow-e'en Sensation at Gov'ner Dering's,
  The* (book) 107
Halloween Weight Test 115
Hallowmas 12–13, 21, 46
Hallowmas Cake Song, A (song) *10*
Hamlet (play) 155
Harper's Bazaar (magazine) 107
Harper's Weekly (magazine) 104, 107
Hartford Daily Courant (newspaper) 111
Harvard Commencement Day 25
Harvest Homes 94
Hastings, Henry 43
Henrietta Maria, Queen (England) 45
Henry VIII, King (England) 22
Hermeticism 43
Hiawatha 26
Hirst, Sam 27
Hoodoo—*See Vodoun*
Houdini, Harry 157
Houston Chronicle (newspaper) 129
Huckleberry Finn (book) 88
Hudibras (poem) 78
Hudson, Henry 44
Huguenots 24, 39
Husking Party, The (print) 55
Hyde, Edward 155

I

If I Were a Man I'd Shoot Myself (book) 107
Industrial Revolution 21, 66
I Need Thee Every Hour (hymn) 62
Institor, Heinrich 31

Ireland
   Divination traditions of 8, 71–77
   Emigration from 66–67
   Ghost stories of *69*
   Jack-o'-Lantern traditions of 77–80, 90–91
   Trick or treating in 67–71, 77
   Victorians and 104
Irving, Washington 60

J
Jack-o'-Lanterns
   Contemporary 141
   Ireland and 78, 90–91
   Victorians and 111, 113
James I, King (Great Britain) 32
James II, King (Great Britain) 39
Jamestown (Virginia colonial settlement) 22
Jesuits 47
Jews and Judaism 38, 42, 51
Johnson, Lyndon B. 149

K
Kale-Pulling 72, 80
Kelly, Edward L. 130
Kelpius, Johannes 43
Kentucky 80
Kissing the Blarney Stone 115

L
Ladies Home Journal (magazine) 107
Lair Bhan 67
Laveau, Marie 85
Lawrence, Eleanor 112
Lee, Charles 112
Lee, Ralph 151
Leeds, Daniel 43
Legend of Sleepy Hollow, The (short story) 60
Lilly, William 23
Loch Ness Monster 153
Longfellow, Henry Wadsworth 26
Louisiana 88
Love Lies A-Bleeding (book) 107
Love's Seed-time and Harvest (book) 107
Luther, Martin 14
Lutherans 14, 24, 42, 45

M
Mad Max (film) 150

Magazines and Newspapers 96, 101, 104, 131
Malleus Maleficarum (encyclopedia) 31
Marcos, Imelda 152
Marinette, Wisconsin 133
Martin, R. Chris 150
Mary II, Queen (Great Britain) 39
Maryland 21, 45, 67
Masks 149–151
Massachusetts 56
Massachusetts Bay Colony 21, 25–36
Mather, Cotton 34
Mather, Increase 27
Matrimonial Advice 115
May Day 27, 28–29, 40, 59, 75, 116
McNeill, F. Marian 61
Memorial Day 135
Mennonites 39, 42
Metamorphoses (poem) 6–7
Mexico 94
Midsummer Night's Dream, A (play) 82
Mirror Divination Traditions 73, 75, 113
Mischief—*See Pranks*
Mischief Night 61, 71, 143
Mormons 57
Morse, William 33
Mozart, Wolfgang Amadeus 150
Muck Olla 67, 80
Muster Day 25

N
Newark, New Jersey 124
New Britain, Connecticut 131
New Hampshire 21, 25, 36
New Jersey 41
New Mexico 93
New Rochelle, New York 129
Newspapers—*See Magazines*
Newton, Massachusetts 135
New York City 124
New York State 21, 39–41, 80
North Carolina 45–46, 88, 91
Nurse, Rebecca 34
Nut Crack Night 57, 63
Nuts
   Celtic traditions and 56
   Colonial traditions and 63
   Irish traditions and 72
   Roman traditions and 7, 57

O

Oberlin, Kansas 126
O'Bryan, Ronald Clark 143
O'Bryan, Timothy 143
Occult
  Massachusetts Bay Colony and 34
  Pennsylvania and 43
  Slavery and 63, 83
  South Carolina and 46
  Virginia and 23
  in Western States 93
Odilo of Cluny 11–12
Opper, Emma A. 109
Osis, Karlis 153
Ovid 6
Owls 89

P

Palmistry—*See Chiromancy*
Pandora's Box 63
Parades 151
Parents' Magazine (magazine) 145
Parlor Games 113–116
Parris, Betty 34
Patrick, Saint 45
Penn, William 41–42, 44
Pennsylvania 21, 42–44, 80
Philadelphia Times (newspaper) 116
Physiognomy and Chiromancy (book) 23
Picus (Roman god) 7
Play Parties 52, 53–56
Plymouth (Massachusetts colonial settlement) 27
Pomona, Festival of 14
Pomona (Roman goddess) 1, 6–8
Pope's Day—*See Guy Fawkes Day*
Pork Night 36
Possibility and Reality of Magick, Sorcery, and Witchcraft, The (painting) 3
Powder Plot Day—*See Guy Fawkes Day*
Pranks and Mischief 61–62
Presbyterians 24, 51, 80
Protestantism
  Colonial America and 21
  Guy Fawkes Day and 14–16
  of Massachusetts Bay Colony 25
  Reformation and 14, 22
Puckett, Newbell Niles 83, 88

Pumpkins
  Irish traditions and 65, 77–80
  Victorians and 119
Puritans
  American Revolution and 51
  and Catholicism 33
  and Colonial settlement 21
  of Connecticut 36–38
  Maryland and 45
  of Massachusetts Bay Colony 25–36
  Rhode Island and 38–39
  Witchcraft and 32

Q

Quakers 24, 38, 41–42, 45, 51, 67

R

Rawson, Grindell 27
Reformation, Protestant 14–16, 22, 42
Rhode Island 21, 25, 38–39
Roman Catholic Church
  All Saints' Day and 8–14
  All Souls' Day and 8–14
  American Revolution and 51
  Colonial America and 21
  Early traditions of 1
  Georgia and 47
  Maryland and 45
  New York State and 39
  Puritans and 25, 33
  Reformation and 14, 22
  South Carolina and 46
  Victorians and 104
  Vodoun and 85
  Witchcraft and 31
Roman Empire 8–14
Roman Jr., Phillip 43
Rutman, Darrett B. 24

S

Saint Valentine's Day 41
Salem Village (Massachusetts) 31, 34–35, 157
Samhain (Celtic Lord of the Dead) 2–4, 67
Samhain, Festival of 2–5, 8, 14, 44, 71, 113, 154
Santeria 85
Scavenger Hunts 119

Scotland 1, 8, 80–83
Sewall, Judge 27
Shakespeare, William 82
Shrovetide 47
Silvanus (Roman god) 7
Skeklets 80
Slaves and Slavery 46–47, 60, 63, 66, 83–85
Snap Apple Night 56, 63
Snow White and the Seven Dwarfs (film) 137
Society of Friends—*See Quakers*
Souling 67
South Carolina 46
Spinning, James M. 129
Sprenger, Jakob 31
St. Nicholas Magazine (magazine) 105
Starkey, Marion 34
Star Wars (film) 149
Stuyvesant, Peter 40, 44, 155
Sutton-Smith, Brian 145
Sylvester II, Pope 12

T
Taman, Festival of 6
Teackle, Thomas 23
Tennessee 80
Texas 93
Thanksgiving Day 30, 53, 63, 142, 158
Three Luggies 57
Tituba 34
Tostan, Kevin 143
Toy Manufacturers of America 145
Trick or Treating
  Charity and 146
  Contemporary 135, 141–143
  Guising and 44
  Irish traditions and 65, 67–71, 77–80
  Roman Catholic Church and 12
Trott, Chief Justice Nicholas 46
Turner, Tina 150
Tylenol 145

U
UNICEF (United Nations International Children's Emergency Fund) 141, 146, *147*, 149

V
Van Arsdale, Johnny 155
Vandalism 124–131, 133
Vertumnus (Roman god) 7
Victoria, Queen (Great Britain) 86
Virginia 56, 80
Virginia, Colony of 21–24
Vodoun 34, 85–88, 93
Voodoo—*See Vodoun*

W
Wall Street Journal (newspaper) 150
War of the Worlds (radio broadcast) 158
War War II (1939-45) 131–133
Water Test 38
West Virginia 80
Wightman, Francis P. 88
William III, King (Great Britain) 39
Williams, Roger 38
Will-o'the-Wisps 78
Winter, Thomas 15
Witchcraft Book, The (book) 46
Witch Dungeon (museum) *144*
Witches and Witchcraft
  Colonial America and 22
  Connecticut and 38
  and Festival of Samhain 2–4
  Laws against *32*
  Massachusetts Bay Colony and 31
  Pennsylvania and 42
  Puritans and 32
  Rhode Island and 39
  Roman Catholic Church and 31
  Salem Witch Trials 34–35
  in Scotland 81
  in the Southern States 87–88
  in the 20th Century 152–158
  Virginia and 23
  and Vodoun 85–88
  Water Test and 38
  in Western States 93
Wizard of Oz, The (film) *136*

Y
Yarn-Winding 75, 80
Yeats, William Butler 57
Yoruba 85